Barack Obama
and the
Road to Bondage

A Case Study

Barack Obama
and the
Road to Bondage

A Case Study

by

R. M. Catton
and
S. W. Catton

This book is not a work of fiction, and any similarity between the persons cited herein and any real persons, living or dead, is fully intended.

Dedicated to those Americans who have always been proud of this wondrous nation, and thus sustain it so.

"All Socialism involves slavery."

— Herbert Spencer (1820-1903)

Acknowledgments

The makings of this volume are diverse and varied in origin but collect themselves into four groupings: friends, family, the news of the day, and the transcribers. The news of the day stands on its own merit and is known to all in its reach. It need not be cited farther. Friends and family were often the proving ground of an entry's general relevance and palatability. Such sore duty so well served funds our deep and lasting gratitude.

The transcribers deserve special note. Their loyal, steadfast, and often advisory effort resulted in the transformation into right and ready text the raw, untidy scribblings we, in our rôle as final common pathway of unrendered, barely legible notes funneled forth to them. One such stalwart is Mrs. Gail Basca Neubling who recast most of the early scribblings into more workable print and then tended to the seemingly endless text re-workings which followed. The other scribe is Mrs. Myrna Knaide of M-K Computing Services, long veteran to our other literary efforts, in her rôle as formatter and general factotum for all the innumerable things which need to be done for bringing a text to camera readiness, as we feel this offering now is.

We, all of us, send this volume forth to the kindly tolerance of the readers in the hope that they will find value in our collective effort.

RMC
SWC

Table of Contents

Prologue

This book was not planned or configured from some *idée fixe*. Nor was it, like Athena, sprung from our heads fully formed and prepared to assume its position among its ilk, needing only to be committed to the printed page. No, it began as our shared and gathering disquiet over the path our nation seemed lately to be taking. There had been, of course, other times over the years when we felt concern and even dread of certain national trends and drifts as they descended upon the American scene, and especially so when such trends and drifts were underwritten by questionable legislated policies and programs. At those times we wondered what had become of our collective societal and political compass such that we had reason to wonder what was driving the unsettling changes and what was setting our direction, and to where. But for the most part we attributed our concerns to the humble and quite peripheral position we held as ordinary citizens, bit players in the massive currents of social and national necessity pacing the collective weal along, and that we, among the smallest divisible parts, could well expect to be astounded, and dismayed, by the play and tumult of Titanic governmental forces as we occasionally came to glimpse them. We consoled ourselves with the conviction that those forces, even when infelicitous, were fundamentally of, for, and by the vital spirit driving the American way of life. So a certain forbearance and patience seemed in order. After all, some change was key to the very process of growth and development.

But several years ago change assumed a different character, or so it seemed to us. Previously it had been handmaiden to the furtherance of American exceptionalism and promise, and all citizens were free to find their rightful place in that common pursuit as their talent and energy allowed. But the "new" change spoke more of equality in terms of parity and likeness, not of equality in opportunity, the traditional mainstay of American enterprise. Policies and programs mandating enactment of this "new" change, which perversely removed individually-driven change from the repertoire of personal ambition, now came forth with ominous and pervasive portent, enacted as it was by a Congress now seemingly dissociated from the preferences of the people, certainly in itself a "change," and indeed a doctrinaire sea change, though hardly miraculous or propitious, but truly strange.

It was at this point we, SWC and I, appealed to each other for thinking beyond our ordinary ken in hope of coming to terms with what we feared was creeping across the land. The winds of "change" coming out of Washington were blowing fitfully and carried a chill disturbingly Socialistic in aspect. We were as mindful as anyone else that command economy had failed throughout history wherever attempted and that its advocacy continued only in the splendid isolation of college faculties and in the desperate economic exertions of woefully backward nations. And we wondered why it was surfacing in the richest and most advanced nation the world has ever known. Or why it was that the populace seemed so blithely tolerant of such dangers befalling them. We dreaded that we were witnessing an insidious national malady. Our dread soon hardened into outrage that the simple, even credulous, trust the American people placed in their elected leaders could be suborned into a witless obedience to a dissembling officialdom, not to mention the threat being mounted against our now targeted Democracy, moreover that such was being blandished along by a shameless and co-opted media. The "what" which was happening soon became evident enough, but the "why" of it persisted in our disquiet. We felt goaded into finding a voice to bring such abominations forth to fuller view for diagnosing the etiology of the national distemper. And our friends and family were the first to be scourged by our effort.

It soon came to our attention that we were not alone in our task. Others had sought to be heard, pro and con, and had sallied into Cyberspace to prosecute their cause. It seemed to us that the Blog had become the public means of personal expression, especially in political and social causes, since there was no longer any faith left in addressing letters to the editor or to our elected officials who seemed astonishingly well-to-do in form letter replies. So we, too, undertook to visit the Internet. It then became a matter of organizing our discussions around discrete themes cast up by the events of some given moment, trim them to a handily readable size, and post them as Blogs. This we did as themes arose in our discussions which themselves arose and formed as daily events directed. There was no overriding or organizing plan directing the selection of topics or their sequence; we simply recorded our discussions as daily events shaped them, summarized them into compact entries, and committed them to our Blog site. And we did so over the course of several years.

We had no preconceived idea how many Blogs we would offer, or what if any conclusion they would yield. But eventually we noticed that the sequence did indeed suggest a causal, organizing factor at play, a not so invisible hand, one might say, and that, as such, some meta message was afoot and on its way to revelation. It was about this time we began to wonder that, if such were the case, could these Blogs be compiled in book form; a different kind of book for sure, but one which indeed had a story to tell and would do so by way of a series of abbreviated, condensed discourses on separate, distinct issues, the bearing of each upon the other being left to the art and craft of the reader. In a word, a series of bricks with the connective mortar of fluent construction left to the reader and his particular predilections.

We thought it was worth a try, and so we offer these Blogs as the raw material of our ranging dialogues of the past several years. We recommend them as useful expedients for granting form and content to the swirling currents of today's social and political surround.

We hope they will in some small way help the reader ride the political whirlwind and even, perhaps, assist him in directing the societal storm now so troublingly at hand.

RMC
SWC

I

Definitions

Just what to offer as the starting point of a discussion, any discussion, is not only a typical concern but a suitable one as well. Mercifully, not all starting points need be so prime as the masterful linchpin Euclid postulated as the basis for the development of his Geometry. To wit, a simple point, hypothetical, indivisible, and so deceptively simple. But even a much more modest starting point should adumbrate what is logically and likely to follow from it. Hence, it is good policy to select one which, in its yet unexpressed innards, carries the seminal ingredients of the very discussion it presages. So, our starting point should be a topic not only ripe, but also one ready for the picking. Moreover, if any discussion so delivered is to be valid issue it should tender the frame to shape the contributions of the discussants. Hence, the frame—that is, the *form*—should subtend the elements of the discussion, the *content*.

For the purpose at hand our discussion will speak to the sobering question as to how did we as a nation come to the predicament we now see as a telling portrait of our daily society. It follows from this question that our starting point should promise a large enough canvas to accommodate a societal landscape formed and shaped by the cultural, the economic, the political, and the historical determinants of life as we Americans are now living it. In other words, how did we come to be the Americans we now are—the *content*—as we busily flesh out the metes and boundaries of the nation we have come to be—the *form*.

The starting point we suggest is *Race*. Our nation has been celebrated as a democratizing melting pot, though the actual degree of interracial melding suggested by that appellation has generally not transcended basic genetic lines, save perhaps only somewhat socially,

1

economically to a measurable extent, politically most energetically, and historically least of all. Caucasians still flock together at the preferred exclusion of others, as do Orientals, and certainly Blacks as well. American Indians have assimilated to a notable degree except for some hold-out pockets and enclaves. But for the most part the races remain distinct and enduring, the separate gene pools usually protected by custom, taboo, religion, and sometimes even law. The result is a variegated social landscape, but one now concentrated in the unity of a single nation and not, as formerly, dispersed and conveniently accommodated by separate continents or regions as geologic time had earlier provided. So much for the history of it.

But given all that, there is still the natural drift toward conflation of the races. Plus, it is generally agreed that inter-breeding as well as cross-breeding must have played a seminal rôle in the history of hominid development. Truly, then, the fact that racial cross-breeding is widely resisted at all seems appropriately to be the larger question. The answers are likely legion, but perhaps the chief one has to do with innate differences, *enduring* innate differences, which protect the identity as well as the separateness of the racial groups despite the sustained influence of shared society and common circumstance, thus negating in large part the homogenizing effect of enculturation.

Let's take a nation—a shared environment—which declares all of its citizens, despite race, to be very equal, or at least so under the law. But as we know, racial differences resistant to enculturation often tend to translate into political slogans, especially if those differences breed conspicuous, racially identifiable social and economic gravities endemic to some particular group. The law, very broadly and generously interpreted, says this really should not be. Worse, if those social and economic differences continue to exist despite vigorous and concerted political as well as social effort aimed at their remediation the differences sooner or later crest into a political urgency. We as a nation seem to be at that point today. We know this to be the case when even our daily parlance is policed in enforcement of politically-driven meanings and preferences to guide the use of words designed to discount unwanted racial differences that can't be legislated away or bribed into conciliation.

Race is today a highly charged word and it is to be handled very much as one would hazardous waste material. Accordingly, not having it around at all would be best. But it remains in our lexicon nevertheless because it is a genuine referent to a very visible and troublesome reality resistant to the usual blandishments and dis-semblances typically used to color over societal unsightliness. Next best would be that the word *race*, if it is used at all, function as a univalent descriptive shriven of all possible negativity and rendered wholly positive in its meaning. It should be reserved, we are advised, for denoting only commendable and desirable attributes of persons or groups, especially those persons or groups seen wanting in some other way. But because its use has become just that tendentious and thus so vulnerable to misuse one must be all the more mindful of possible hidden negatives evoked by its use even when best intended. This shaded pedigree has a drizzle effect on its unfortunate cognate, *racial*. We all know that it is dangerous indeed to refer to any personal or group trait as *racial* unless it is done in an unassailably complimentary manner. One could likely get away with referring to excellence in basketball as racially driven, but even that could carry tremors of implied incorrectness, therefore probably making its avoidance best in the overall. And goodness knows that to refer to violent crime as racially driven would be a transgression of irre-deemable magnitude. So the use of *race* as a qualifier is truly a tricky business even when one attempts to give exclusive and praiseworthy credit where rightfully due. Hence, *race* is best not noticed at all, much less mentioned, no matter what the obvious demographics of our society may be.

Except in the political arena. Here, *race* enjoys a ready and handy utility by way of its other cognate, *racist*, and its more generic sister, *racism*, neither of which can claim any redeeming features in their usage except in the designation of evil-doers and their practices importantly held responsible for certain regrettable chronic ills and injustices bedeviling our society. The effectiveness of such usage lies in its ability to mobilize guilt and electoral fervor for the legislation of remedial social programs as additive to similar programs already enacted, regardless what the cold demographics might caution. Such is societal blame and the means by which it is assigned.

But why blame, and for what? Essentially blame for unfavorable differences between one racial group and another wherein those differences are seen as penalizing the one over the other. But why blame, since differences, some indeed unfavorable, do exist not only between racial groups but between individual members of a like group, though blame is not accorded salient status in the dynamic of that setting; after all, Fortune never seems to favor everybody equally. The more telling point is that blame can carry, when needed, the notion that unfavorable group differences associated with race are the consequence of an unkindness levied preferentially on the members of one racial group for the specific benefit of another. Thus it is assumed that a certain bias corrupts what would otherwise be the equal and natural flow of society's commodities to one and all, and that any discrepancy or deviation seen in that distribution cannot be the product of simple circumstance but rather of wicked design; not of innocent, impersonal process but of rank sin. Thus, blame naturally proclaims guilt.

But what guilt? The guilt, one may presume, of having deprived some persons unjustly of the right to Life, Liberty, and the Pursuit of Happiness while that right continues to be guaranteed to others. As it happens, there is, in truth, no lack of historical evidence to support such a charge. The historical evidence is there and the canvas we now paint of ourselves cannot ignore this dark period in our history anymore than it can any other. The grim shading this rude fact continues to cast on our societal renderings is before us at all times, so much so that enormous effort, thus far shy of legislated financial reparation openly designated as such, has been mounted to bestow upon the offended group preferred opportunity for garnering compensated status among its oppressors, even to the point of grossly favored affirmation. Decades have been dedicated to this pursuit—reparations of an oblique sort and thus electorally less offensive—with a vast treasury expended but with little corrective change coming of it. The cries of *race, racist, racism* continue to season the air as reasons are sought to explain the lack of hoped-for gain, even in the face of singular national success in establishing the problem as the rightful concern of all. In this regard, all our social and political endeavors are now mandatorily subject to the litmus test of racial bias.

But what actually are we testing for? It would seem that racial discrimination might sum it up adequately. That's what we hear as the rallying cry of those feeling abused so. But is that really correct? Racial discrimination in itself may simply not be enough to support the charge of wrongful deprivation. Bias, particularly racial bias, may not actually, out of hand, be a flaw or misdeed. But how can that be, in view of all that is said of the social and economic ills supposedly come of it? Let's look at it this way. If as coach of a basketball team we're biased in favor of recruiting Black players, so frank a bias could be seen as sensible indeed because Black basketball players have shown themselves to be superior to others in that sport. Such a racial and recruiting bias would be sensible because it's their game. Look at the demographics. Correspondingly, as coach of a swimming team any bias we may have in preferentially recruiting Caucasian or Oriental swimmers would be just as sensible. Here, the Caucasians and the Orientals have shown themselves to be the superior performers. Again, look at the demographics. We're acting on bias, racial bias, in either case, but we likely would be seen as recruiting sensibly and even properly. So how could it happen that our sensible and approved racial bias might spill over into mis-behavior? Only if we applied our bias unfairly, either way. For example, if we recruited Blacks but didn't allow Caucasians even to try out for our basketball team. Or, if Caucasians were correctly allowed to try out but yet we categorically discounted their skill and

5

rejected them in favor of Blacks of lesser skill simply because we didn't like having Caucasians around. Our racial bias would then indeed be culpable. The same could apply to our decisions about swimming team recruitment, try outs, player selection, etc., were we to follow similar reckoning at the expense of player merit. We would not only be at grievous fault but likely also a losing coach. The essential point here is *fairness*, not bias or discrimination. Heaven help the coach who has no biases or does not discriminate. If such is his lot, he has lost sight of the game and its purpose. He would be a coach in name only, and the only way he could possibly escape the charge of grave misfeasance were if all players, potential as well as actual, be exactly alike in all ways such that he could then attribute his selections solely to chance. Very unlikely. Plus, all players deserve to be recognized for their skill and effort, or else why bother to keep score? But a quite acceptable practice could be that he *preferentially* recruited Blacks, honestly believed them to be man for man superior to others on the court, and openly made no bones about it. And he could avoid the charge of racism, maybe, by keeping team membership open to qualified Caucasians, Orientals, American Indians, and their various blends, the deciding issue for team membership being solely player merit. A disgruntled Caucasian hopeful might yet feel unfairly rejected and undertake some recruitment of his own, specifically of some kindred activist group eager to enforce his claim. He would not likely be inclined to recognize the lack of merit either in his claim or in his athletic ability, much less be willing or able to weigh the issue strictly on the basis of open fairness because in such cases the complainant has usually already made up his own mind on the matter and typically with the wholehearted assistance of his activist contingent. Thus, he would see the coach's selections as racially skewed, which in part would be accurate, but that's likely all he would see, discounting as he would any evidence of fairness being the overriding theme in player selection. And thus in this player's mind the coach would be judged a *racist*. But, in effect, by accusing the coach so, the disgruntled Caucasian hopeful would be confessing to his own racism which he was projecting unfairly on to others.

Needless to say, we all discriminate. We discriminate between up and down, strong and weak, good and bad, competent and incompetent, fair and unfair, and, yes, Black and White. The ability to discriminate is one of the building blocks of human reasoning. Accordingly, it can just as readily and appropriately be applied even to the management of a swimming team. It can also be demonically applied to the drift of current-day America. The charge of racism is a politically handy device, and, coupled with the existential guilt of the culturally more successful races it grants those claiming foul an advantage over those who might perceive their success as coming at the expense of others, for, after all, if one team wins, the other team loses, however level the playing field may be or the sincerity of the effort to make it so. Yet, is it ever really level no matter what? More on that to follow.

Thus the tipping point in any discussion of racism is *fairness*. If all participants in an enterprise are bound by the same rules, and performance is judged in accordance with those rules applied equally, then there is no actual racism regardless of what the players and coaches may think of each other. But opinions? Probably many. Grievances, probably innumerable. However, performance is the issue and fair assessment of merit is the goal, not the salving of wounded sentiment or the practice of a cynical appeasement.

Unfortunately, our political climate is such that its vested forecasters and managers are loathe to have racism lose its place in the armamentarium of partisan ideology. But, actually, when have they ever been good sports?

11 April 2009

II

Policy, Purpose, Personality, and Patriotism

We hadn't intended to broach this particular subject until we were significantly farther along in these entries which, as proposed, were to follow empirically and sequentially from the opening statement and the previous entries. It had been hoped that any topic, such as this one, along with its several relevancies, would logically and necessarily derive from the thematic elaborations of its predecessors, such elaborations and their particulars serving as introduction to subsequent entries' eventual arrival. But that expectancy presupposed a similar, gradual unfolding of societal events as would confer a timeliness on this as well as on the other entries as they evolved. However, of late, societal events have not kept the timetable anticipated but have raced ahead to command pressing discussion far in advance of any concordant thematic preparation offered here earlier. Hence, it could perhaps be said that this entry along with the national moment it addresses, is time out of joint.

The national moment to which we refer is Barack Obama's presidency, and the accelerated pace to which we allude is that of his policy enactments thus far demonstrated and pursued. For example, it has come as a surprise to many that there has been such a rapid expansion of government along with a frightening readiness to spend prodigiously, literally trillions of a yet unfunded future in the financing of that expansion. But to some it is more soberly seen as an opportunistic playing out of a vaulting misalliance between a cresting national fiscal crisis come of managerial malfeasance and the prosecution of an ideology veiled in the blandishments of campaign rhetoric shaped to address popular fears and entrenched jealousies. And perhaps now to an enlarged audience it has become clearer that in times of dissatisfaction and distress it is one thing to think of

9

launching oneself off a precipice in hope of soaring to new horizons and quite another thing actually to do it what with the inevitable and irreversible loss of zeal and optimism sure to come. It can be imagined that such a person, having made his decision and leaped, hurtling down and reconsidering belatedly as he gained lethal speed, that he really hadn't intended for his decision to take him in this direction. Now, as a captive of freefall, it would be his task to make the best of it and hope for a livable landing, despite what the laws of gravity might have to say about it.

There is no shortage of commentary to the effect that President Obama has undertaken to give this country a makeover to shape it more socialistic. The expansion of our government in the sectors chosen seems geared for just that undertaking but the word "socialism" is carefully avoided by his team. There is so much more available commentary on his doing this for the purpose of "changing the face of America," as the phrase runs, relating as it does to a broader social engineering for making the distribution of this nation's wealth more equitable. No matter that a large segment of the electorate who voted for him earlier would not do so now had they then been able to discern such intent embedded in his rhetoric; their need earlier to fly to dangers they knew not of was far too urgent and blinding. All manner of speculation has arisen as to why he is so intent on re-forming America. Besides, widespread popular umbrage certainly is taken at his appealing to other leaders of the world for enlisting their condemnation of earlier behaviors of this nation of which he now happens to be the Chief Executive. His courting such support has, in some cases, placed him cheek by jowl with foreign leaders who have long established themselves as enemies of this nation and who believe America should be punished for its exceptionalism. President Obama's personal grievance with America seems to transcend by far any grievance this nation may have against its sworn enemies, and his sentiment in this regard seems to be so much more kindred to that of our enemies than it is congenial to the security of this nation. Regrettably many of our commentators who proudly hail our exceptionalism, rather than condemn it, tend yet to miss the point, because what they offer as defense of this nation's uniqueness is exactly what so many other nations of the world see as the basis for their grievance. Simply, we've done too well and are too commanding on the world stage. President Obama has assigned himself the role of leading those nations in pressing their claims against America. Indeed, he sees his calling as providing leadership for balancing the distribution of the *world's* wealth just as he seems intent upon doing within the domestic scope of this nation. That task, of course, calls for a significant enlargement of his job description as President of the United States. But he apparently feels that his destiny, not just a credulous electorate and certainly not the nation's Constitution, mandates such, and that not only is it desperately needed, but, in his thinking, long overdue.

Likewise there is no shortage of commentary as to why he is intent on such. The conventional answer is that he just doesn't like America as it is presently constituted. Whether this is necessarily and sufficiently the case remains a daily staple in the national debate. However, we do know how his wife feels about this country, and she is joined in this estimate by his mentor and by so many of those with whom he earlier allied his interests. But little searching discussion is given by those commentators as to the 'why' of his dislike of the nation of which he is now the Chief Executive. Perhaps such a discussion is covertly regarded as unspeakable, though it's alternative—the marking of his presidency as historical in the affirmation of this nation's founding ethic—is seen as more importantly to be featured, though with the word "Black" carefully avoided except in its use as a grand qualifier for the unique history being made in his ascension to the Presidency.

We know that President Obama had a Black father and a White mother. We also know that he was reared largely by his mother's family in a White setting. His schooling was typical White middle class though flavored with the affirmative action benefits mandated those of his Black status. And it certainly is no secret that despite his half-White genealogy and the heavy predominance of White influence in his development he's considered Black; perhaps not as Black as some, such as his wife, but Black still. The point is that conventional thinking assigns him Black status, not White. We do not hear that persons who have a touch of White in their predominately Black genotype are considered White. Not at all; they're considered Black. And we do not hear that persons who are predominately White but have a trace of Black in their blood are regarded as White. No, they're regarded as Black, too, unless they've successfully crossed the color line. The implication is obvious: anything less than pure White is seen as belonging to the race of the other contributing component in the genotype. This notion extends to other blends as well. A White and Yellow mix is seen as "Eurasian," which actually is not either, but a Black and Yellow mix is still Black. The same applies in part to the Red race. It is also obvious that being pure White—or Yellow, or Red—is held to be the desideratum, and that anything less is regarded as miscegenation at its best and mongrelization at its worst. This seems to be the built-in thinking of at least Whites—Whites anywhere, not just in America. The cosmetic industry and the plastic surgeons do not anywhere have a lot of business among Whites and Orientals, least of all among Blacks, in making them look Blacker or more Negroid. Quite the opposite, though some Orientals have opted to look more White. That's simply the way it is and one doesn't have to look far for examples. Thus the tendency is to regard persons of Black and White mix as having a flawed pedigree, either way, and that persons who are ostensibly racially pure in their genotype are seen as more genuinely who they are, again either way. It is suspected that this applies as much to Black thinking as it does to White, though the advantage is seen to lie with the White race since Blacks are generally not widely welcomed anywhere except in their own native homeland. At least, not anymore. And that also simply is the way it is.

Given all this We believe that President Obama dislikes, perhaps even hates, being Black. And We think that this is the basis for his disliking, perhaps even hating, America. And these sentiments might be shared by the mixed persons in his life—his mentor, some of his associates, and even his cabinet members, not to mention some other prominent Black activists of this nation. But why so when their White mix has perhaps assisted them in achieving the prominence they have? This infelicity might perhaps explain in part President Obama's preference in selecting second and third world leaders with whom to ally himself in mounting a critical judgment of America. It may also help to understand his assumption of a peculiar global stance in his stewardship of our nation. More on that later.

Thus, the question arises as to how his dislike of being Black can translate into such a driven dislike of America when he has reached, by way of all the opportunity this very nation guaranteed him, the zenith of colossal and generous personal success as proof of this nation's founding ethic. A touch of treachery at play?

12 May 2009

III

Passion of the Self

Our previous entry ended with the question as to why President Obama's dislike of being Black should transpose itself into a hatred of America. Certainly his pronouncements here and abroad have made it clear that he is opposed to America as it has been. This opposition cannot be rooted in our nation's generosity to other nations of the world, or this nation's energy and enterprise in rebuilding other nations devastated by war, strife, disease, or famine. Nor can it be because this nation almost alone has stood available to feed those peoples their own governments could not. Nor can it be because this nation has provided the lesser nations of the world with the encouragement as well as the template for social, political, and economic growth. It also cannot be that this nation has espoused the principles of democracy and the glories of freedom to peoples long alien to those blessings. Nor can it be that this nation totally alone has long held out the hope to literally tens of millions who would come here in search of the fulfillment not possible in the lands of their origin, or even elsewhere. No, We don't think that these particulars could be the reason, unless President Obama is of such a perverse nature as to condemn compassion, charity, and generosity. We can't imagine that he is, but the issue could be more a matter of who it is being charitable, generous, and compassionate, and to whom. The Scots have a saying: "Do a man a favor and he'll ne'er forgie ye." The cynical truth of that cautionary piece of advice may bear closely on our question.

It is certainly known that favors may take many different forms, and also that the same favor to one might be regarded as something quite different to another. For example, doing a favor for someone who is fully equal to exploiting its benefits and often you get a grateful beneficiary and usually, in time, one who is again productive in life's pursuit though he might, still and all, feel remiss that he needed a favor in the first place. His sense of obligation for receiving the favor might rankle him perhaps even to the point that he never forgets a certain debasement that came of his having needed it and received it, and so never really forgives his benefactor. Even so, he usually gives credit where credit is due and tailors his gratitude accordingly. Entire nations as well could have such sentiments.

But grant a favor to one who is simply not equal to the opportunities which that favor promises, and let that person's failure to exploit those benefits be much too clearly seen, and soon those benefits, needing to be sustained for lack of the recipient's ability to secure them on his own, are regarded as entitlements to be continued. There seems to be a basic truth in this: some people are truly unable to care for themselves in an advanced, technologic society and hence become members of a custodial class which is to be cared for by the other more successful members of that society. Again, whole nations as well could have such limitations. And sentiments.

It all may simply be a matter of the difference between being poor and being broke. People who have always been poor, even only comparatively so, are a lot less likely to know where benefits should take them and so will remain pretty much where they've always been but perhaps more comfortably, while people who are simply broke tend to have a much better idea of where they're going or should go, given the means, because they've been there before. The poor never have.

The difference is readily seen also in some of our minorities and subcultures. Some people arrive at these shores after years, even generations, of oppression and abject poverty in their native lands and immediately seize the moment this nation offers to set themselves vigorously at work in exploiting the opportunities available. Their children are encouraged to use education or commerce as the ladder to success, and in one generation those children are on the faculty of the schools they earlier attended while others have their

16

own firms and companies which then hire working Americans. And they remain minorities and often still with a certain measure of alienation from the mainstream.

But, as we know, there are others, often minorities as well, who seem inadequate to the opportunities and encouragements this society may offer. Many of them also have a history of oppression, even enslavement. These people, although long ago manumitted, claim a certain compensatory preferment still being extended for the purpose of underwriting and encouraging their overdue and actual attainment of status at least equal to others in the general mainstream. But we know that such has not been the result with as many as wished. Moreover, most of those who have not progressed are Black. Here the underwriting and support tendered them over the past fifty years seems to be regarded by them simply as due reparation and entitlement. Hence their thinking seems to be more of receiving the preferment rather than using it. Yet some Blacks have indeed used it to great personal advantage, but they seem to be a limited sub-group among their own kind.

So what must the difference be between those energetic and enterprising recent émigrés and the notably less progressive but long-established minorities of this nation, primarily the Black minority? The answer appears to lie in a fundamental difference in Culture Capital, as some have called it, even by some very notable Black scholars at that.

Culture Capital may be described as a group's collective capacity and innate tendency to establish the style and the structure—the form and the content—of their historically rooted societal cast which extends back in time as far as generations are counted. It is a cast that is carried somehow in the wiring of a kindred group only to be played out more fully in the aggregate form by group effort. It would be easy to call it an instinctual bent but then there would be the corollary problem of explaining how such a bent is acquired. But acquired it is, and successive generations seem to fix it more firmly in place as though from a practice effect accompanying the process

17

of group adaptation, while that very practice, in turn, adds to the innate structure itself as would an additional brick mortared in place in the ongoing construction of an edifice. The individualization of such practice is seen in the family unit as a mini-culture derivative of that family's larger culture. Thus, Culture Capital connotes the breadth and depth of what the group has generated in the art and science of life as the group has lived it and has sustained it over generations. How it becomes genetically established and transmitted as a partial instinct, introjected as an inheritable tendency all of its own, is not understood, but it is understood that selective breeding can achieve decided proclivities, as fanciers and breeders of domesticated animals will attest.

It goes without saying that Culture Capital is then like money in the genetic bank and it underwrites the group's establishment and operation of a life style: its goals, practices, and the all-important ability *to view itself*—all collectively known as its "culture." And some groups are innately richer than others, and usually for demonstrable reasons in the history of that group's traverse of its existence, with climate and geography certainly making large contributions to the mix. For example, the lowliest peasant of Asia who has labored in the rice paddies for generations, usually paddies belonging to another, and living in a wattle, one room hut with a thatched roof, little formal education if any, and long a prisoner of his simple and primitive lot, carries yet in himself the limning of the cultural achievements of his larger society. His language, his religion, and his awareness of what is there for the accomplished of his kind though beyond his personal reach, constitutes a world to be cherished and desired, if not for himself then maybe for his successors. He would have some sense of what is possible of his kind and what his culture embraces because there is a codified history of his people recorded durably in their own language by persons such as he to serve as a conduit for providing succeeding generations a transcendent cultural imago mere word of mouth, ephemeral as it is, could not advance. Writing, which presupposes an alphabet in its most efficient form and pictograms in its less developed form, is the handmaiden not only of cultural solidification but likely is also an additional means by which the development, feedback fashion, of those partial instincts which incline a group adaptationally this way or that is fueled. The lowliest olive picker in Italy grew up in the neighborhood of Caesar, Dante, Michelangelo, daVinci, and was thus subject to their broadcast effect.

Regrettably the Black race is the poorest of all the races in this regard. It has no alphabet or written language other than what it has borrowed from other races and their cultures. It has only relatively recently, and not at all widely, begun to transition itself from animism and magic to a deistic religion which also is borrowed from more advanced cultures. Its native tools and implements of daily living offer no advantage in a modern world, and the tools and implements now available and necessary for living in a modern society are not of their own invention but, again, are borrowed from superior cultures. Their native art is limited in scope and is primarily ceremonial in design and purpose. Native music has been little more than the phatic rhythm of the tree trunk drum, and its contribution to modern music preserves that generic rhythm but now with borrowed instruments for digital fidelity. Its literature, for lack of a written language, never rose above word of oral legend, and social organization never advanced beyond the tribal. A sense or conception of "nation" embracing different tribes in a larger common identity never evolved, and the national boundary lines drawn on the map of Africa, especially in sub-Sahara Africa, were drawn by superior cultures, not the natives themselves, except in only the most recent cases, and they too tend to trace tribal boundaries.

Most of the Blacks in this country are the descendants of sub-Sahara Blacks brought here by the slave traders during the colonial and the ante-bellum days of our history. In many cases those early Blacks were drawn from the lesser African tribes and sold into slavery by other more dominant tribes and by traders from the Muslim world.

Those slaves arriving at these shores were confronted not only with the wretchedness of their status as chattel, but also with a society whose cultural riches were never known to their primitive tribal existence and whose equivalent they would not likely have achieved independently on their own for many thousands of years. Their cultural wiring had not evolved nearly so far, and certainly not to the point of spawning a civilized way of life unlikely to come to them of its own for many generations, perhaps many thousands of generations. Being left totally to themselves would assuredly have guaranteed just such a timetable. The issue is a regrettable one and essentially so because so vast a number of primitive Black people were removed from their native environment and from their own kind and inserted into another, much more advanced culture in which they could not fit. The adaptation gap was too large to breach, at least for many if not most of them. More on this later.

"... for many if not most" is the key idea. The implication is that some did, and do, breach the cultural gap and even quite successfully but probably never totally except at the expense of renouncing their primal genetic loading. And few can or do, except the line crossers. That's why one sees prominent members of the extended Black community in this country embracing and even becoming leaders in forward-reaching, predominately White movements as part of their political affiliation but, when the moment arises, only to vote for a Black opposition candidate espousing Black preferment. The tribal and racial wiring runs too deep. However, it is well known that Whites will vote for their Black candidate though the opposition candidate is White. The thinking here is more national, not tribal or racial.

Given that circumstance one can readily appreciate the fractious position of the Black man in a White or Oriental society. His cultural underpinnings are still significantly influenced by his hunter-gatherer culture style while the White or Oriental cultural thrust has moved on to the complexities of civilized community organization.

20

Therefore, rightly or wrongly, the Black man placed in such a setting is confronted with a personal crisis far beyond that of Whites and Orientals transplanted in each others cultures. Despite the differences in language, life style, and practices between Whites and Orientals the wiring tends to be similarly developed.

Faced with such a crisis the Black man is forced to address both aspects inherent in any crisis: opportunity or ruin, gain or loss, and the inevitable pragmatic blend of the two usually in some balance consistent with sustained personal identity.

And this brings us back to President Obama.

President Obama embodies two distinct racially contending elements, both physically and psychically, in a blending of two cultural archetypes but with one prevailing over the other. He presents so much more convincingly as Black rather than White, and his wiring, though blended, seems to oblige him more to the purview of the generic Black man in America. Such a posture, likely a consequence of his father being pure, unadulterated Black, appears to transcend even his early White upbringing and his mixed parentage basic to his conception of himself, and does so in obedience to the conventional reckoning of such blends (see Entry II). Thus, President Obama appears to carry within his daily being the challenge of fitting the underpinnings of one culture with those of another for achieving a salubrious blending, if possible, in the grounding of his personal identity.

But usually, such blending is not so salubrious, because the Black man is naturally reluctant to accept the inevitability of a subordinate position in the world's line-up of cultures, much less the notion that the difference between the Black man's stage of cultural evolution and that of the White's and the Oriental's has more to do with innate, genetic wiring, much like intelligence, and not with the predominately standard contention citing societal circumstance as the cause, such as poverty, the heritage of slavery, or prejudice, all of which are actually more consequential than causal. Also more on that later.

21

For the Black man it's a challenging existential circumstance, compounded by the likelihood that because of the difference in basic wiring and capacity, aggravated by his protective denial or even defiant refusal to see such, only the Whites and Orientals, even if themselves not wholly independent of self-service, are yet perhaps the only ones able to understand and approach this issue dispassionately. The blending of Black culture with the more advanced cultures then perforce becomes more a matter of providing a means of accommodation, not a matter of achieving a unified identity. Certainly the differences come of superior avocational skill and the consequent disparity in reward and wealth are open for all to see with the more advanced cultures thus established as the sustaining, providential benefactors, but, yes, also the abusers of the less successful cultures which, at their worst, are then seen as merely custodial participants in the workings of the world. Legislation and funding can be utilized as a means of constructing a humane accommodation but neither method can honestly or rightly be seen as addressing the root cause of such custodial status, though the dependent cultures would wish it simply to be so and thus call the matter an imbalance correctable by a majority vote or widespread redistribution of wealth. But such a misconception, despite the oft-shown and inevitable default awaiting its political enactment, may actually gain a certain credence if advocated aggressively enough and class envy is stoked in kind.

The situation described thus is cosmically tragic, cruel, and unsolvable by civilized means if racial identity is to be sustained. It begs for generosity, compassion, and policy as only the superior cultures can provide and endorse, plus a certain realistic re-definition of components of the problem for concentrating the potential effectiveness of any remedial measures.

We think this circumstance besets President Obama not only in the task he feels is asked of him as Chief Executive but also in the reconciliation of contending elements of his very own identity. His givens are not exclusively of the superior culture, nor exclusively of the subordinate culture. Nor are his fundamental religious beliefs those of the mainstream of this nation, or even of the Western world, the leading nation of which he now finds himself President. He is thus not completely of the scene over which he presides. Therefore, he has a certain detachment and quite likely a unique personal view of this nation and of his responsibility to it. It is suspected that this view does not limit him to the observance of his job description mandated by law, but yields him a sense of mission come of his personal problem with race as well as his identification with the global problems of similar cast but which are, perhaps, conveniently at hand in a more manageable size by way of the distinctive circumstance of the United States of America, the only Western nation with so sizeable a long-endemic Black community. It is also the only nation with the resources needed for approaching such a problem. And it goes without saying that the rest of the world watches as America searches its social and political landscape for a viable solution, a task which faces the entire world, now and soon, with formerly distant continents becoming close neighbors because of modern commerce and technology. The unspoken hope is that if there indeed is a viable solution it will be found in America by dint of its power, its wealth, and its egalitarian democratic traditions.

Thus, it is considered that President Obama not only sees himself as the very embodiment of the problem but the solution as well. In his conception of himself and what he believes has been his success in achieving integration of his own personal identity he sees a prototype, a model of what should be the path of a multi-cultural America, and the world as well. His decision, if such it be, derives of his recognition that he cannot be more White than he is, no matter what his effort, since he will always be nominally and manifestly Black; and any hope of his being otherwise would be a doomed and hapless pursuit, subject to the derision of both the Black and the White camps. Plus, a compensatory working at being more Black could not override his White genetic loading or his essentially White upbringing. Moreover, because of his father's foreign nationality he lacks the necessary credentials for being authentically American Black. It then seems his "choices" feature his blend as a special providence for leading this nation to a kind of social and political salvation which the rest of the world could then follow, just as large parts of it did, or attempted, with America's ongoing demonstration of the virtues and benefits of an egalitarian Democracy. Thus it appears he feels he has a unique, even ordained global mission, and along with it the conviction that he is precisely the one chosen for it. And it appears he is singularly determined to prove such to himself as well as to everyone else. Essentially, the mission requires that America, and likely well beyond, be re-shaped in *his* own image. This notion of having transformed a dreadful adversity into a compelling virtue would help to explain not only his recent innovations in the structure of our government for the redistribution of wealth— the minorities to be the primary beneficiaries of such—but also his recent world travels for enlisting the participation and support of other nations, especially second world nations, to include those whose religions are resonant with his own for the fuller exercise of his ministry. The more advanced cultures, the habitual winners in the culture race, are to be compared to athletes on contraband steroids and are to be penalized for their unfair advantage; and the lesser cultures, like unprepared and underage participants in the exploitation of technology and science, are to be favored with having a larger participation in the achievement of equality in the Deliverance promised. It is this Deliverance, to be initiated here in America, which is President Obama's actual agenda, not the protection of the Constitution of the United States in keeping with the job description designed by the nation in its founding. To him his personal job description appears to be a calling which overrides constitutional law and comes from elsewhere and beyond the reach of Americans and their Congress which just now appear so readily compliant.

Hence, it appears that President Obama is more in alliance with a world view likely more kindred to that of nations which have America as its sworn enemy and whose downfall is their strategy

24

separately as well as collectively by way of their envy or their religious imperatives. Though he is the Chief Executive of a nation which elected him by virtue of its success in transcending tribal and cultural biases, doing so in keeping with its founding principles, President Obama seems determined to change America from what it has so successfully been into an entity permissive of the very practices and policies the American people eschewed in its founding. The founding proclamation guarantees freedom to the individual for his pursuit of happiness in recognition of God-given individual differences as the vehicle for that pursuit, but now those gains are to be regarded as unfair if resulting in an imbalance of material success. To that extent President Obama is at war with the America that elected him and he seems to offer more hope to its enemies than he does to the larger population of this nation. Much has been said of the detrimental effect many of his policy enactments have already had on the infrastructure of this nation and its citizens, and pleas have been made to bring such to his attention as excessive, regrettable, unintended consequences. But if he is genuinely at war with this country as it presently is, and that certainly does appear to be the case, he is likely quite aware of the collateral damage his policies cause and will cause, and he also likely regards that damage as a measure of success in his overall agenda of changing the face of White America. In effect, the more he destroys the more that can be rebuilt in his own image. The cries of consternation and disbelief that such damage could possibly be unnoticed by him truly come of missing the point entirely. President Obama actually intends such damage as necessary to the prosecution of his war, and he is supported by an enabling and unscrupulously opportunistic political party while the opposition party is disabled and cowering. The American people are left with the task of allowing themselves to realize that they have put in the White House someone who is intent upon winning his war against their nation, subduing it to the satisfaction of its enemies and those who have long envied its success and power, and changing it into something few can now imagine and which would never have been founded in the first place for freedom to thrive as nowhere else.

It is often said that Americans generally spend so much more time deliberating on what kind of car to buy than they ever do in deciding which candidate to vote for. The conventional, merry reason given for the difference is that the people pay for the car with their very own money while electoral follies are paid for by the government. Or so they think.

12 May 2009

IV

Gift of Prophecy

Our last entry called attention to President Obama's conviction that his personal identity is destined to serve as the template for the reformation of this nation in achievement of a new identity of its own for adjusted relevance not only to its citizens but also to the other peoples of the world. The mission he has undertaken seems to require executive enactments and policies which extend beyond the traditional authority or duties of this nation's executive office. It was also mentioned that such an agenda was likely based on his privately held belief that his mission is an ordained one empowering him beyond what is embraced by executive mandate defined in the founding document of this nation. Plus, it was suggested that his mission was kindred to as well as enabling of political forces which hold that the best founding charter for a nation's governance is one which supports and actively facilitates governmental participation in the daily affairs of its citizens, rather than one which carefully restricts such. Lately, much has been said and written as to whether our Constitution is too negative and that it impedes national as well as cultural growth because of singular imperatives largely seen in its amendments which openly undertake to harness government securely to the protection of individual liberty and states' rights. But it is equally held, and with the support of tradition, that the government should never, in the protection of this nation's special virtue, become one which harnesses the people to its own purposes. The debate continues as to who should be guiding whom—centralized authority or individual freedom—and for what purpose? The Progressives tend to regard our founding document as simply an administrative aid for the implementation of agendas derived of a conception of this land as they alone envision it to be; to wit, a government which shapes the cultural life style of its citizens in satisfaction of its conception of the proper needs of those citizens with all such priorities established primarily by the government itself. The Constructionists however, tend to regard our founding charter not only as the very centerpiece of their life style but also the daily guarantee of personal liberty whereby the people, in more individually responsive forum, are enabled to define their own needs as well as the means of satisfying such, and do so in the exercise of their individual rights and freedoms with the charter setting discrete limits on all elected authority. Hence, a broader distinction between the two outlooks is that the Constitution is to be adjusted to suit the policies of government as opposed to the government being adjusted to suit the mandates of the Constitution. One posits governmental authority as conclusive; and the other, individual freedom as more basic. One features security and regulation as defined by government, the other advances personal liberty and enterprise as defined by the electorate. One approach establishes a central power less restrained by guaranteed individual rights; the other a collective governing power derived of guaranteed individual rights practiced in forum. Thus, with one the individual is defined as the servant of the government, and with the other the government as servant of the people.

As it happens, the American people, to the extent they understand and appreciate these contending issues, are divided on this point. Moreover, their electoral behavior is not always consistent with what they hold to be their civic values; personal need and fear often trump their claimed principles when the time comes to choose their electors, and this conflict may represent in microcosm the larger political debate which occasionally has been described as the enduring challenge presented by the divisive demands set by the Reality Principle and its waiting temptress, the Pleasure Principle, both of which are operant in each of us at all times. More on that later.

President Obama's approach to government clearly favors the centralized control position, and it is considered that this may well be so because he readily sees himself as a unique expression of that larger debate. How? He may perhaps see his arrival on the scene as providential with entitlement to a special personal freedom by which he exempts himself of constitutionally mandated limitations such that he may preside over the contending elements of this debate and see them as merely derivative, perhaps even moot, while demonstrating his own exempt personal liberty, but conversely in the service of central governmental control, effectively his control

But how can this be? If, in his effort to change government design, he draws upon a special personal freedom, a freedom exceeding the mandated limitations of his office, and does so with the automatic obedience of a compliant majority party, how can that very design reasonably be in favor of less personal freedom for others and more government control of options available to the electorate? Clearly he must hold himself above the very ordinances of the government he authors. A certain sovereignty is implied and he appears to see no contradiction at play in his role.

But how can he do this, and with seeming unquestioned entitlement? And justification?

While there may be active debate about the fixity or the flexibility of the Constitution, or about protecting its integrity as opposed to proclaiming its malleability to suit social circumstances, there is yet general agreement that it still is actually the basis of our governmental process. The notion of not having a Constitution, or of rescinding it as an instrument of government and allowing it to be relegated to mere historical significance is not touted as a conscionable consideration. The Constitution is what it is: the founding and declared doctrine of this nation; this nation's very definition as proclaimed by its founding citizens. It is this nation's ontologic as well as its political existence captured in writ. It is what gives this nation its very name, and you would no more change its constituted identity than you would change a person's name in compliance with style or trend, as does seem to be the practice in the entertainment world; or worse, allowing no name at all because being nameless effectively removes one from bothersome relevance, perhaps even accountability. As with the Constitution, so with this nation. What would America be from day to day, year to year without the Constitution's accrediting presence? Likely a sequence of resemblances changing with each administration and with every national or global challenge, and having no nodal point for doctrinal or ideologic orientation. What kind of credibility would such a nation have?   That nation would be seen as embracing a kind of programmatic anarchy, unpredictable, and evanescent on demand. But it would provide very keen staging for a leader wishing to display a transcendent and sovereign control in providing direction and purpose for a populace who would now be more like subjects than enfranchised citizens. And it would no longer be First World. More on that later, too.

Despite the all too human pull for personal aggrandizement and whatever the specific and personal psychological forces unique to any individual experiencing it, the capacity and drive for discounting the revered founding document of this nation, a document regarded by the world as one of the most compelling and enduring statements of political idealism and human endeavor ever seen, a document copied by many nations in their effort to rise above primitive and totalitarian status for the pursuit of liberty and happiness, such a capacity and drive must derive of some very consuming and impassioned design not only long in ferment but also vengefully malevolent to America as we know it.

We also know President Obama has circumvented, if not violated, many basic tenets of the Constitution and especially the spirit of checks and balances those tenets call for. He seems to feel his policies and programs are exempt of the executive restraints observed by former Presidents, the most recent offender rightly cited juridically and held publicly accountable for his transgressions. But thus far, not President Obama, except by those brave souls who continue to violate the frank embargo on public airing of his repeated malfeasances.   But the fact that many people and his apologists exempt President Obama of the restraints applied to other Presidents speaks not only of a special accommodation accorded him by the news media, certainly by his party, and for now by a majority of the electorate as well, speaks even more tellingly of his sense of readiness to exploit that accommodation in demonstration of his contempt for this nation's founding manifestoes, and primarily our Constitution.

It's one thing to use an accommodation such as he enjoys in extension of this nation's commitment to provide encouragement and opportunity to a sector of our community previously disenfranchised by fiat—such accommodation the general population can endorse, at least up to a point—but there comes a time when performance is to be judged by the requirements of the job and not excused or obliged by way of preferment. In this regard, affirmative accommodation must need be seen primarily as a means and not as an end in itself, as never was intended. Perhaps. Be that as it may, one can yet expect President Obama to be granted a generous abetment in his performance as our very first Black President, else his detractors and critics be categorically seen as, and publicly accused of being racists (see Entry I). But in that abetment it quite likely was not intended that he violate the codes and principles of the nation granting him its highest office though abuse of such accommodation, graciously and even penitently granted by the populace, and certainly never extended other holders of that office, is exactly what the Constitution purports to prevent. Thus, we see another demonstrated example of President Obama's intent to efface the Constitution's reach.

So could this be the basis for his open misprize of the very document which establishes and defines his office and especially his relationship to our governing process? Maybe, but his agenda seems even more fundamental than the polemic over the fixity or the adaptability of the Constitution and just exactly what was intended by its framers. His program enactments disregard the Constitution's guidance, its spirit, and even its political existence. Hence his enactments bespeak a fundamentally different view of the Constitution from what is held by its citizens, or at least the vast majority of them, both parties. The result is that President Obama seems to be governing from a position not recognized by either the Constitution or the full electorate. And what can that position be?

Totaling it all up, it appears that President Obama regards the Constitution and likely also the Declaration of Independence as White racist documents born of a White racist society for the sole benefit of Whites and the perpetuation of their society. Certainly it is true that these documents were penned by White men for a White society which held Blacks in bondage and denied them the rights and freedom therein granted Whites. Thus, he may well see those documents as reminders of a White attitude more basic than even the documents themselves, despite transformative amendments come of a bloody upheaval in the nation's redefinition of itself along with its relation to its Black population. Nevertheless, no Blacks participated in the Constitutional Congress or in the formulation of the Declaration of Independence. None. Yet it is also true that even if the Founding Fathers were gifted of so sublime a prescience to know America as it is today they still would not have found it feasible to have barely domesticated, much less civilized, slaves participate in the creation of such elegant coinage. Indeed, the difference between the cultural level of first generation Blacks of then and the societal position and cultural advancement enjoyed by their descendants today is a clear measure of the degree of success this nation's manifestoes and national spirit allow, encourage, and protect. Most Blacks know this, even if grudgingly. There is little traffic in Blacks emigrating back to Africa. The direction of flow remains today as it always was and perhaps even in the case of President Obama himself, though he nevertheless perhaps regards the Constitution as enduring and clear evidence of this nation's innate evil, the evil of being a guilty White society now making some attempt to undo and perhaps color over its unforgivable wrongs. Such thinking is rooted in "Presentism," the fallacy of assessing past meaning and blame on the basis of the standards and perspective of today. Yes, it was cruel to burn heretics at the stake, but the people back then truly believed that the immortal soul of those benighted unfortunates could be saved no other way. Should the Christians of today be punished for such behavior? Or the descendants of the victims receive reparations from the Christian world? Certainly President Obama's mentor feels this way in regard to past slavery, and even his wife has suggested as much. So to him the Constitution is to be seen not as a noble and revered document transcending its time and generative of the world's greatest nation unto this very day but rather an instrument of evil for exploiting vulnerable peoples in its drive for aggrandizement. A smoking gun, so to speak. It is said his Kenyan father felt exactly this way about European settlers in Africa. Thus, the Constitution, he may feel, is more an enemy not only to him personally but also collectively to Black America as well as to other peoples of the world. Hence his continuing apology to the other nations of the world for America's very existence, much less its behavior. He is thus not the Constitution's or America's advocate, but their reformer. The Constitution is to be circumvented whenever possible as long as it remains in effect, for to abide strictly by its tenets would be to endorse it, even to champion it, if only obliquely; a kind of giving aid and comfort to an enemy.

His role as reformer thus presumes his vision of change to be more transcendent and moral than America's present governmental process though that process is already some two hundred plus years in operation with the accomplishment of enabling this nation to become the greatest ever known to this world, and granted as such in just about all reckoning. Plus, charitable beyond comparison.

But if the Constitution is to be circumvented, whereof comes his job description and his role? It must arise of his own conception of himself and of his role at this given time not only here in America but in the world at large. It also presumes a prescience even our Founding Fathers could not know. With President Obama the dimensions of his design certainly exceed the political identity and daily workings of this nation, certainly that of other nations as well, and suggest that the design very likely approaches the realm of Prophecy.

It may well be, and indeed does seem, that President Obama sees politics and power as mere enablements for the recognition of his chosen—not elected—status as the Prophet of the new meaning of nations, the change to begin here in America where his being President is truly the lesser part of it, but strategically crucial. The role of the Prophet is not at all alien to his founding catechism, but it is perhaps more to the point that the Black Race, though fervently yearning and seemingly always in the process of preparing itself for the advent of one, has never had a Prophet of its own; only White or Yellow ones, perhaps a point of reproachable Culture Capitalism, one might say. Perhaps the epiphany of President Obama's socialism just might offer some redress of that baleful wrong.

07 July 2009

V

Crime and Punishment and Beyond

The previous entry addressed President Obama's executive posture as more that of a Prophet than a President. In the former, his relationship to our government seems that of one who is encumbered by an archaic system which places unacceptable restrictions on his ministry, obliging him to accommodate a doctrine and protocol which, when not convenient to his personal goals, is best circumvented. But those very restrictions are present by design, specifically articulated by our Founders as unabashedly fundamental to the framing of the Constitution just so. The restrictions are in no way unintended consequences. Yet, there has been more recently a tendency among some of our Presidents to honor their constitutionally defined role and its limitations so much more in the breach than in the observance, as mentioned earlier, with emphasis more upon their pursuit of personal agendas than upon guardianship of the Constitution and the derivative governmental process. Too often this has brought about a division in thinking with the result that partisan lines are drawn in seeing the restrictions as either vitally necessary protections against the use of tendentious power for levering a national regression into governmental autocracy, or else are held to be bothersome archaicisms which now have little place in the fulfillment of a modern leader's vision. The intended checks and balances system is designed precisely to prevent just such a turn to self-serving pursuits. But an ongoing and infelicitous consequence of just such a polemic results inevitably in any given President's being either a friend and protector of the Constitution, or an adversary and opportunist intent on bending it to personal need. In a larger sense, the former is aligned with the task of overseeing the governmental process as was intended and instituted, while the latter is given more to the exercise of convoying personal policy through the legislative process and, if necessary, at the expense of the integrity of constituted governmental principle and procedure. In the former, the President holds himself more responsive to the actions of the people's Congress, and, in the latter, more directive of such, should partisan accommodation be adequate.

And the latter is about where we are today.

The partisan accommodation President Obama enjoys offers a broad range of possible pursuits. However, he seems to focus almost exclusively on the domestic issues of the day. True, his appeal is global, in view of his many visits to foreign capitals to register his responsiveness to their interests. But his embassy, in sympathy with those interests, does not feature this nation as a generous leader but more a contrite one bent on conciliation and change. In keeping with such, his recent fiscal enactments at home and his advancement of government into the private sector do strongly suggest that the exhaustion of the national treasury is quite compatible with, if not germane to, having America assume a distinctly modest national posture more in keeping with that of so many other nations of the world. America's exceptionalism is not to be advanced, but rather more a compensatory consanguinity, perhaps even a retributive parity. The image suggested is more that of an America falling contritely in line than it is of an America pacing economic and technologic growth for other nations to behold, benefit from, and perhaps even strive to emulate.

But why would President Obama want America, in forfeiture of its pre-eminence, to become just one of many nations? Our former Presidents, save one, have been strong advocates of the nation of which they were Chief Executive. It seems implicit in the role of President that effort be directed at the enhancement of this nation's global position, not the abridgement of it. In fact, the gauge of Presidential success and greatness seems linear to the success and greatness of national achievement under a given President's term.

Indeed, the national disposition in large measure directs the President's energies and defines his effectiveness.

So why would President Obama undertake to achieve a lessened America, lessened in global standing and lessened in overall domestic life style? The standard shibboleths, such as unfairness, man-made global warming, wealth inequity, ecology, energy, etc., are generally enlisted as dignifying reasons. But these are not particularly creditable or even credible reasons for they could quite successfully be addressed with America's exceptionalism intact. They are merely trendy rhetorical devices, much like slogans, electorally useful as contrived obliquities, even pseudo-issues, to be used as a basis for enacting legislation in fulfillment of more covert agendas which otherwise would never pass public muster. No, it seems evident that President Obama wants America humbled, and, to be sure, not at all for reasons of national or international enhancement of status; rather, such humbling has to be for reasons specifically his own and for his own purpose. It cannot be said that he is acting on the wish of the people that all—the nation as well as its citizenry—be led in assuming a condign humility. True, there are some among us who would indict this nation's power and pre-eminence, such persons as those seen in his Cabinet appointments and staff, but they in no way represents the majority of the citizens or their devotion to this nation. Nor their pride. Thus, President Obama's conception of the matter has to be otherwise. As said, his approach and policy seem punitive in nature, and certainly many around him echo this intent. And one doesn't have to look very far for telling reasons. This nation's history, specifically that part dealing with slavery and subsequent oppression, bears witness to a lingering grievance by the Black sector and no less the regret of Whites that it indeed did occur. The Whites of today, affirmatively committed, are innocent of the transgressions of that past just as the Blacks of today are strangers to the transgressions of that same past. True, many Blacks still harbor grievance over felt abuse, but the issue may not be so simple as suggested by historical fact. It may be more what slavery revealed about the Black man, just as hatred reveals much about the person of its possessor. More on that later.

So President Obama may feel that this nation should be taken to task for its past behavior, and that this reckoning should occur in witness of other nations of the world on the premise that this nation's attitude toward them and former abuse of them as well demonstrates its continuing need to oppress others for the purpose of its own enrichment. That would seem to account in part for the penitential cast to his foreign policy. And it is clear that he feels he is the one to see that such penance is done. But we suspect there is much more to it than solely America's just deserts being played out on the global scale. We think President Obama does see himself as a Prophet, at least so much more a Prophet than a mere office holder, albeit the highest in the land. And, regrettably, his presumption may indeed be the better part of his unique conception of his elected purpose. All major religions have their own Prophets to show the true way to the faithful. Certainly President Obama's religious leanings embrace a faith renowned for its Prophet, the faith itself eponymous in that Prophet's name. And of course there is the philosophical question as to whether whole nations, even the collective world of nations, like individuals, have within their doctrinal identities given destinies which carry the hope of national salvation as well as the threat of existential damnation. A secular faith, so to speak. We think President Obama, in the role more of a Prophet than President, intends to lead this nation in expiation of its sins to achieve a kind of national salvation. So much of what he sees as America's evil would thus have to be destroyed in the process, and his vision would serve to light the path for leading us away from the America we've known.

Yet, to do so he first has to be beyond mere natural citizenship in this nation, and that may already be an accomplished fact, and hence moot. Perhaps. In order to be a credible Prophet, he has to show that he is uniquely different from and beyond the mainstream of this nation's people. And that also may well nigh be settled, for otherwise he might be judged simply a spokesman for this nation's

38

re-aligned interests though only more global about it. Rather he must be seen as the Reformer of this nation and thereby also credentialed for serving other nations in the same capacity for achieving a global amity and peace, especially for the Black man and kindred other minorities. In a word, he has to be different in order to do the different—and be handsomely credited for it. Thus his advocacy moves well beyond his instituted function as President, and his actions transcend the normal restraints come of the checks and balances normally practiced by the three divisions of our government. Accordingly, in his vaulting approach to office the distinction between religiosity and legislative zeal is subtly effaced.

It seems to follow that deep within himself President Obama does indeed see his way as the way of the Prophet but one whose Book simulates *Das Kapital* for the teachings needed to "save" his people. Even though his rhetoric is rich in such words as "change" and "create," and his mission laudable in the limited sense, he still cannot, no matter his approach, "save" his people because of the flawed and fundamentally imperfect distinction between cause and consequence in the admissible specification of that task, which, by its very nature, is regrettably unsolvable, at least in a civilized, fiscally feasible, and socially tolerable way. Treatable, yes; but curable, no. More to come on this point as well.

August 07 2009

VI

Winners and Losers

We have seen that President Obama loathes America as a White Racist society and discounts its founding documents as little more than White Racist charters favoring the perpetuation of just such a society. Though the documents make clear notation of their fundamental principle of the equality of man, they also mandate that such applies in practice only to the bona fide citizens of this nation in their lawful dealings with each other. The documents do not extend this status and privilege to non-citizens or to others of foreign lands. Thus the only acceptable meaning as to the intent of these documents is that they are to be known as instruments of governance, national in scope and application. They were not, or sensibly could be, intended as devices for formatting social design. Whatever the philosophical validity of the proposition of equality as promised in the documents, it is clearly intended to apply only in a juridical sense and is referrant only to the citizens of this nation.

However, others have entertained the notion, and have argued, that since the founding documents pledge obedience to the credo of equality, their application and enactments have thus far served too insular a purpose. Some hold that if the documents truly be our guide, the universal truth of our founding credo should then oblige us to an equally universal application in our dealings with our fellow man, and we should thus extend to all, domestic or foreign, enfranchised or not, the benefits and blessings now enjoyed by American citizens as the sole beneficiaries of those documents. In a word, some hold that the documents rightly should extend beyond mere governance of this nation and its bona fide citizens but have as well a global reach in our dealings with other nations and *their* citizens, especially those on our soil. Our national document is now to be seen as a global one, if we are to be true to our own credo, it could be said, and is said.

While such thinking may offer a seeming logical reduction, it is clearly not what our founders had in mind. Our governance style was indeed intended to guide our commerce with other nations and their peoples, but it was not intended to confer on all others the rights and privileges enjoyed by Americans. Other nations might take their guidance from this nation in establishing governance similar to our own, but the welfare of their citizens remains their responsibility. The Universalists think otherwise, even to the point of illegal aliens being given the opportunity to vote in American elections, and enemy combatants being granted the rights and protections of the juris-prudence designed and instituted for American citizens. In the process, America forfeits the sovereignty embraced and established by the founding documents and thus assumes a more communal status in the world of nations, subject to the rulings of that commune.

This departure from the founding national intent seems to hinge on the very tendentious, if not cynical, use of the word "equal." Simply, America is to be more "equal" to the other societies of the world. American exceptionalism is thus unacceptable because of its violation of the principle of transcultural equality. In its most con-crete and absolute sense, the concept of equality requires that all men be created the same: height, weight, etc., even color—a patent absurdity. Individual differences continue unabated. A less concrete use of the term "equal" requires that all men are to be "seen" as created equal though not actually so, thus a certain departure from the comprehensive spirit of the matter but a departure decreed necessary in establishing a starting point for formulating a workable national charter. Now, the qualifier "seen" comes under review along with the companion referrant "equal," with the result that absolutist thinking demands that those obdurate individual differences, which ordinarily would merit reasonable and fair acknowledgement, be discounted as significant in societal make-up and character. A more temperate view of the matter would recognize the notion of "equal" as a doctrinal device allowing men to be "seen" so, but not at the expense of real individual differences which might even be embraced as useful accessories to national advancement. This view would rest on the premise that "equal" would be subtended only in the doctrinal sense; specifically, "equal" only under the law. We could then pursue our fortunes, enjoy success in accordance with our energies and talents, choose our society according to our individual taste and do so without being in violation of national policy. In a word, we would be free. However, it is well known that Universalist-Absolutist thinking holds that freedom, and its applicability, be geared more to national, even international, pursuits and not to the uniqueness of the individual as has been our history and the engine of our commonweal. Thus the individual would then be less the driver of the national apparatus but more a passenger to a destination likely less of his design. In this sense Freedom would not be seen as a natural given to be experienced legally by the individual as wished, such as height and intelligence, but as a condition defined and allotted by government. And thus the individual would not be born free; he would be born property of the government and his use would be determined by such.

It is fairly certain that the framers of our Constitution intended equality of man to apply only under the law, the common man to have the same rights and privileges as did the nobility, even the royalty of the day, with enfranchisement of all the citizens of this land being the important first step in that enterprise. As stated above, citizens of other lands stood well advised, but obliquely so, to consider a similar approach in their own governance. However, the de facto institution of such governance would have to be undertaken by the individual nations themselves. America as then constituted, did not see itself as the plenipotentiary of the world with all the world's people as citizens in various degrees subject to its political and moral suzerain. Not in any wise. Perhaps only *in potentia*.

But certainly not then. The framers of our Constitution took it as a given that the nation they gave birth to could be nourished and sustained only by an *educated* and *godly* citizenry. Indeed, these were the unspoken requirements, collective as they were, for those included in that congress of people to be known as the citizens of America. Native Americans and Blacks were thus unqualified, though the former less so, but each on the basis of cultural lack of a deistic religion which resulted in their continuing reliance on animistic magic and charms for spiritual expression. Moreover, they could not provide of themselves an enabling education, specifically an education that included an achieved, endemic system of notation to support reading and writing beyond primitive glyphics; no alphabet, no codified pictograms, and specifically no approach, however modest, to the classical Western European education which spawned the very Constitution itself. In other words, a lack of cultural elements of mentation beyond primitive tribal thinking, elements considered necessary for comprehending, much less embracing, the concept of "nation" and the responsibilities of enfranchisement. These people were thus seen as inhabitants, not citizens, and certainly not by fiat or by number equal to men of White European cast. They were regarded as primitives, not quite arrived at a cultural level of development to qualify as being civilized, but rather, if living in a White society, simply being domesticated at best. More on that later.

Such seemed to be the societal backdrop to the use of the term "equal" in the framing of our Constitution. The term applied exclusively to White America as a given recognition, and if it applied at all to the excluded, lesser elements of the societal landscape, it applied, once again, only *in potentia* with the presumption that excluded elements, the mere inhabitants, could, by way of opportunity and application, in time achieve civilized status to stand equal among the enfranchised. But though optimistic and evangelical, was that expectancy flawed as well? It seemed to suppose that all men were fully capable of a certifying level of cultural development in a democratic, civilized society.

As with "equal," this expectancy, even though protected and enshrined by statute, may itself be flawed. As stated earlier (see

44

Entry I) and certainly daily open for all to see, no amount of training, encouragement, support, or preferment can make most of us champion athletes. Such help could likely make us better than we would otherwise be, but it could not override basic modest givens capable of only limited development. Ask any coach, or music teacher, or mathematics teacher. For example, all of us have the prodigious gift of speech to qualify us as *Homo Sapiens*, but even so, and immediately upon that basic capacity, speech patterns and skills vary widely and do seem proof to the influence of enculturation. More on that later, too.

And the same seemingly applies to native intelligence, individual as well as racial. There has been heated and vigorous debate on this point because of the consummate importance of the implications. So much derives of either way the question is held or found. The contending forces are generally grouped into two camps; one addressing measurable intelligence and its normal distribution across groups, and the other discounting any findings which suggest strong differences between racial groups. The latter camp questions the validity of such testing and gives *nurture* a large share of cause in any significant differences noted. The former camp assigns *nature* the primary role in test differences. This camp also allows for the role of nurture but sees its influence limited and not at all decisive. Moreover, this camp holds that differences noted are in those sub-tests measuring skill and innate ability correlating highly with general academic and vocational success anywhere, not just in Western society. Those doing the research testing are satisfied that their tests are valid for what counts in general social and industrial accom-plishment, while the opposing camp holds to the position that test result differences are situational and amenable to social, academic, and economic change. Thus the latter more readily lends itself to a political activism, and also opportunism. The latter also seems not only the more hopeful but also, in a way, more in keeping with the general social tenor of our Constitution, despite the exclusions of its day, but certainly not with the data of current intelligence testing. To

45

this day the gap between fact and fancy in this regard provides an arena for all manner of political and activist mischief, don't we know.

So why the controversy over intelligence testing in the first place? Because the most thorough and extensive review of the field and its findings not only shows that significant racial differences exist but that the differences are fixed despite social, political and educational remedial effort, effort which extends from apportioning primary and secondary classroom make-up to affirmative action policy favoring minorities at the expense of fair and traditional criteria in job placement and for admission into our colleges and professional schools, not to mention the incredible treasury spent in these efforts. But despite such extreme measures the racial differences persist very much unchanged in oblique resolution of the nature-nurture argument decidedly on the side of nature, much as is consistently made clear by testing results as well as by the long-held knowledge come of our daily experience. But it seems our political system persists in search of a nurture-based solution simply because the system is doctrinally incapable of accepting, much less providing, a nature-based approach to the matter. Here again, the confounding effect of the term "equal" and its tendentious definitions—political, biologic, philosophical, legal, and also religious. The issue is a cosmic one far beyond the reach of mere government, but in no way is it a new one to a world that has, and has had for eons, its evolutionary winners and losers, even among the *Homo* genus. Neanderthal man could be specifically informative on this point. But, then again, if he could speak to the matter, or had ever been able to speak beyond phatic expression, he probably would not have become extinct. However, still and all he did last a quarter of a million years under the very same ecologic circumstances as did Cro-Magnon man who is a relatively newcomer to the human scene. Would our current Cro-Magnon-based government have attempted to save him? Most assuredly, since it shows little hesitance in applying its dominion and treasury for the preservation of the spotted owl.

30 June 2009

VII

The Penny in the Dark

We all have heard the fable of the simple, unfortunate fellow who lost a penny in the dark but looks for it in the light where it's easier for him to see. We all can offer a rueful smile at the pathos of such a pursuit, perhaps so in recognition of its broader application to the essential human predicament: we prefer to look for answers only where they are more comfortably available and readily visible, especially if that approach is congenial to some preferred agenda. Examples of such abound throughout the history of man's relationship to calamity, disease, even to the weather. But such quaint folly, especially if innocent and sincere, may have its up side in providing a plausible method in the face of a collective confoundment, though strong evidence of the durable effectiveness of that method might be lacking. True, such an approach, and almost any method, often seems to be, at least initially, a virtue in itself, despite being suspect as to long-term benefit, but yet a virtue and for no other reason than that timely implementation of almost any tactic bespeaks a certain dutiful effort commendable in its own right and likely reassuring for its worthy intent alone. Like prayer, one might say, since it is good to pray though not all prayers are answered, as we know. Yet, keeping the faith that they will be offers a certain solace come of believing that a future ordained by the heavens can be favorably influenced by man. Thus method, any method, bespeaks a tribute to man's endeavor with the gods.

On the other hand, such hope, which serves as the parent of method, implies a recognition of needed earthly action along with a certain exercise of judgment in the designation of some given remedy. Our unfortunate friend not only perceived that he'd lost his penny but also that some solution to his calamity was in order. But not only that, the solution would have to embrace some degree of search, a heated search if necessary. That part of the problem would be seen as straight-forward enough. But the question of where to search remained. He deduced that looking in the dark promised a search more harrowing than that which would be needed for a quick and handy return of the penny to his purse. And certainly a safe return as well, because everybody is afraid of the dark; there's just no telling what might be found there. So a search in the light was the method to be pursued, and if done with fervor and dedication a penny might indeed be found but not likely the one lost; that penny would remain out of daily currency, but the one come of his looking determinedly in the light would be ready for tender. In this sense it might well be allowed that a penny earned is a penny saved.

So it seems to be with so much we do: if our problems demand understanding for the framing of solutions whose meaning and methods would take us to where mortals fear to tread or where the results would not be humanely sanguine, we adopt other more congenial solutions which yield methods easier to apply though they be merely oblique and sometimes even at the cost of aggravating the actual problem. This approach seems to be innate in our political system, perhaps every political system dealing with problems which have over an extended time of varied governance endured as our human predicament. Perhaps politics, the flawed tool it is, is the only applicable one that can be agreed upon, though so often it seems dedicated to misreading enduring problems for the employment of methods geared to secondary, even partisan gain. This state of affairs has given rise to the observation that while science endeavors to provide eternal solutions to popular problems, politics provides popular solutions to eternal problems. Heaven help the political system which does not have an eternal problem it promises to solve, else the system's reason for being would go wanting. Hence such problems are vital to the interests of the generic political effort, an enterprise which has not rarely seen itself the dread enemy of science whose apolitical posture too often fails to appreciate that some human torments such as calamity, disease, and even the weather are to be embraced as political sustenance, and not to be fruitlessly remedied. Indeed, some members of the present Presidential Cabinet have felt the need to remind us of this obligation. Politicians, our experts in this matter, know so much more about this field of endeavor than do we, the simple, credulous electorate who devotedly keep looking for leadership and guidance among the most visible and most available for the quick and handy relief our predicaments demand. Forswear having to look where it's not so comfortable.

Man is the measure of all things, it's been said, and his ideational capacity defines the limit as well as the scope of his experiential universe but with perhaps the promise of more yet to come to his ken. The siren song of hope, don't we know. But because of personal differences in that ideational capacity we, as individuals, live in personally different universes. But we do experience much of it the same way with the overlap establishing the basis for the communal feeling driving the social process. Yet, it is the differences between our personal universes which structure our individual identities and which may account for the poetic longing that comes of harboring an inevitable and essential loneliness.

As individuals vary, so do collections of such. The overlap in which each member of the collection shares with the other may define a distinctive communality and may do so by way of language, dialect, custom, ethnicity, and certainly race. The successive tiers of over-lapping joint membership seem to serve as the bedrock of a given culture and its distinctive stamp. Just as with the individual within each of us, certain elements of a given culture may not be totally communal; important differences may remain and do so in a distinctively defining way such that we have the phenomenon of subcultures varying uniquely within the larger scope of a parent culture. This phenomenon may be all the more operant, and evident, in our nation, America, which sets ethnic and racial heterogeneity as a desired medium for the exercise and proof of a political doctrine which posits the equality of man along with democratic governance as the vehicle for the right to life, liberty, and the pursuit of happiness, the keynote dictum of our collective identity today as Americans, even though not so collective of all the inhabitants of this country at an earlier time.

A prominent aspect of this heterogeneity is race. Perhaps no other nation of the world carries so prominently all four races in the demography of its citizenship. Most nations know only one race, some perhaps know a secondary racial element in the line-up of its citizenry. But not four, as does America, and certainly not as a matter of course. Yet, this proving ground of the equality and communality of man also affords observable differences which endure in the face of a common environment. As would be expected such differences have been studied as markers as well as contributors to the status a given identifiable race may and does achieve in American society. One line of study in this regard is the measure of intelligence and its distribution within and among the races.

This subject is approached with trepidation, and it may be the paramount national taboo. It is, despite the wealth of its voluminous and elegant research, the darkness we dare not explore. Far better, we look where it's more comfortable, or allowed, for explanation of crucial racial differences; at least, the more unpleasant differences. We're sure we've all noticed, individually and collectively, that desirable traits, individual and collective, are allowed to have traceable genetic origins—the proud and wholesome *nature* of it—while undesirable traits, likewise individual and collective, are preferably seen as the product of society—the flawed and fixable *nurture* of it. An entire national and political industry is based upon this common, and perhaps socially essential, predilection. It is perhaps obliquity at its best and hence key to the distinction between science and politics and their conflicting goals. And it also has much to say about our regard and understanding of Truth, whether we see it as a guiding light or a signal of danger, yielding two very different perspectives concerning the darkness around us.

That much said and the metaphor smartly applied, it is time to address the topic of measurement, and especially the measurement of variation. Happily, the field of Statistics provides us with just such a device. As many of you may know, that device is called the Standard Deviation. It measures variation of a particular trait within a sufficiently large randomized group. It traces a normal curve of distribution for that group and carries a predictive value in assessing the frequency of occurrence of that trait. It is based on both the trait's mean occurrence in that group and also the trait's observed frequency of occurrence in either direction from the mean. The mean, or average, performance on standardized intelligence tests has long been assigned a value of 100 for computing the Intelligence Quotient (I.Q.). The standard deviation derived of the measured test scores is 15. The number of standard deviations above or below the mean predicts the frequency any given I.Q. will appear in a sufficiently large randomized group of human beings, assuming randomization to be valid in avoidance of any distortions come of skewed sampling. The conventional values are as follows:

The average I.Q. of Orientals is recorded as 106.
The average I.Q. of Whites is found to be 100.
The average I.Q. of Blacks is seen to be 85.
The average I.Q. of Americans in general is said to be 98.
The standard deviation is continued as 15.

Hence, Blacks are tested as being one full standard deviation below that of Whites and almost one and a half standard deviations below Orientals in measured performance on standardized tests of designated intellectual function, "designated" taken to mean the battery's several sub-tests for assessing capacity in specific skills, such as vocabulary, memory, object completion, and so forth. Likewise, we see that Whites score approximately one-half standard deviation below Orientals on such tests.

Of course, all manner of protest, condemnation, even outrage has been raised over such results and their dissemination; to wit, the tests do not truly measure intelligence but only limited, reachable, and measurable aspects of it; or that the construction of the testing and its results is merely circular and compounds the false assumption of the significant racial difference by basing the referent standards initially on White testees; or that the influence of education and poverty are not accounted for in testing results, and so forth. All these objections may contain an element of validity, and they have accordingly been addressed forthrightly and objectively with adjusted testing methods. However, the same differences remain. Plus, scores on the standard tests and their sub-tests correlate highly with successful job performance and overall adaptation in an industrial and technologic society. Hence, it appears that in view of Oriental dominance and Affirmative Action programming for Blacks an evolving subsidiary rôle for American Whites is afoot in the general academic setting. But let's not look at that dark prospect, yet.

25 August 2009

VIII

Metes and Boundaries

In the previous entry we broached the American taboo forbidding discussion of racial differences in measured intelligence. It is suspected that the standard objections are forthcoming to point out the problem of unfairness, questionable validity, and demonstrated unreliability in such measures. There may indeed be a degree of unreliability in such measures, and there may thus also be objections based on the charge that such I.Q. tests are really White men's tests, developed by White men, and scaled to celebrate White men's perspective style, and then calling it Intelligence. Lest time be spent unprofitably in addressing such charges it can be pointed out that various test scales have indeed been developed to offset just such advantages White men may enjoy come of education, cultural background, more stable home and family environment, nutrition, and even favored financial status. Such adjusted tests may de-emphasize verbal skills and feature motor and visual-perceptual skills since the standard tests have shown that the verbal scale, particularly the vocabulary sub-test, shows the highest correlation with the overall test score and is thus a strong determinant of such as well. However, even when modified tests are given to discrete racial groups the score differential and the standard deviation remain about the same. The notion of comparative intellectual aptitude is inescapable, if one bothers to delve into it. Researchers who have devoted their professional careers to the study of intelligence and its measurement have written consummate books on the matter and yet have generally borne the opprobrium of an offended public, or at least that of a more outspoken sector of it. The criticisms usually follow one or another form; sometimes both are combined. One form tends to address method; the other, motive. The challenges addressing method

53

usually raise questions about the basic definition of intelligence. For example, is there indeed a comprehensive intelligence sampled by various sub-tests, or do the sub-tests, fashioned as they are, specifically sample separate and discrete faculties which, taken together, give the appearance of a comprehensive intelligence? No less than seven separate intelligences have been so defined as making up comprehensive intellectual function.

Those addressing the issues of motive raise questions regarding sampling and the mischief that might be at play in that pursuit. There are also concerns as to the suitability of assigning discrete numerical values to the measured results. Moreover, some challenges, those of a more emotional nature, tend to assign dark purpose to such testing by way of perhaps hidden *a priori* assumptions held by the testers. To such challengers, motive overrides both method and results, and, while obliquely conceding the validity and reliability of the test results themselves, may discount any utility of such findings simply because the offensiveness and presumed insensitivity involved in making such results a public matter far exceeds what is necessary. Human compassion is seen as the more important pursuit, not the divisiveness lying in wait of test scores even though they are shown to be of a given natural distribution. To such challengers, quantifying mental capacity and especially the differences within a group is tantamount to measuring the degree of impairment suffered by those with a club foot as compared to the celerity of those not so benighted—and then calling everyone's attention to the difference unmindful of the effect such would have on its "victim." And worse, done in the name of science. Thus the morality of such testing is questioned.

Hence the impassioned sensitivity surrounding *comparative* mental testing. No such polemic is associated with measuring racial differences in height, though of late some sensitivity has developed over comparative measurement of weight. Not even longevity, for the most part. But intelligence? It's the marquis of distinguishing difference and the reason is that everybody knows that it means just about everything to culture, social progress, and even survival. No one has yet fully come out in favor of abolishing intelligence in preference to an exalted role assigned to faith and feeling as preferred approaches in managing the human predicament. Not for a long time, anyway. But societal desperation may once again well put us close to that day, and soon enough at that if and when no one is allowed to be more cognitively apt, or at least measurably so, than what is seen in the lowest common denominator of our electorate. More on that later.

Not only does the cognitive mean speak thunderingly, but so does the standard deviation as well. The mean tells us simply what actually is, but the standard deviation goes beyond this and tells us what to expect. It's the messenger too many people are happy to shoot. Simply, it is a predictor of the likely frequency of occurrence of any measured trait in a given randomized and sufficiently large sample to yield a normal curve of distribution.

In its predictive value the standard deviation gauges the degree and likely frequency of the occurrence of a given trait within a randomized, sufficiently large group, and it affords comparison of the same trait measured in some other sufficiently large randomized group. The larger the subject groups the better. Performance on standardized I.Q. tests, I.Q. thus defined operationally, is the trait being considered here, and the comparative scores achieved by separate White and Black randomized subjects sees the application of the standard deviation for the comparative expectancy of a given score in each group. For example, *one* standard deviation above and below the mean of a randomized group subtends approximately 68% of that tested population. If the mean of that population is 100 and the standard deviation is 15 then the variation in score for that subtended group ranges from 85 to 115. That's for one standard deviation. *Two* standard deviations from the mean of 100 subtends an additional 28% of the tested group with 14% above the mean embracing scores ranging from 115 to 130 and 14% below the mean covering scores ranging from 70 to 85. The remaining 4% of the tested population is split between a 2% above the mean and 2% below the mean for additional standard deviations each way such that three standard deviations above the mean constitutes a score of 130 to 145 and 70 to 55 for three standard deviations below the mean, both together comprising approximately 4% of the tested population. A remaining fraction is given over to additional standard deviations above and below the mean and yield extreme scores.

The percentages noted here designate frequency of occurrence. For example, subjects within the test range of one standard deviation from the mean will occur 68 times out of a 100 in a randomized group, 34 of them above the mean and 34 below, and so forth. The exact frequency of any score, such as 123 or 92, can be calculated by the applicable mathematical formula. This exactitude is most readily seen in a normal curve of distribution, the "Bell Curve."

Group differences may now be measured and compared statistically on the basis of a given trait's frequency of occurrence in each group, one group having a mean score of 100 for the given trait, and a group having a mean score of 85 on the same trait. For a group with a mean I.Q. score of 100, those scoring in the 100 to 115 range comprise 34% of that group. But that *frequency* of I.Q. range scores occurs more than twice often as it does in the group scoring a mean I.Q. of 85. For the score range of 115 to 145, two standard deviations from the mean, the difference between the two groups is even greater, approximately seven times more frequent in the group having a mean score of 100 as opposed to the group with a mean score of 85. In deviations even farther from the mean, the difference between the two groups expands all the more.

The resulting demographics are notable. In the group with a mean score of 85, the number scoring in the 55-70 range is correspondingly about seven times greater than in the group with a mean score of 100. From a cognitive standpoint, this score range bears on the definition of a custodial class.

As noted above, the Black population is tested as having a mean I.Q. test score of 85 and the White population a mean test score of 100. This of course does not mean that Blacks don't score in the 131-145 test range; it's just that they do it so much less frequently. It also means they have so many more who score in 55-70 test range. For example, for every 100 Blacks scoring in the 115-130 range there are 700 Whites doing so. Correspondingly, for every 100 Whites scoring in the 55-70 range there are 700 Blacks with the same scores..

Hence, this distribution should make a Black man with a test score of, say, 175 a national treasure in view of its great rarity, but it usually doesn't, at least among his own kind. Why?

The reason probably bears on the notion of Culture Capital (see Entry III). Suppose a person with an I.Q. five standard deviations above the mean is born and reared in a simple farming community where merely scratching out a living is paramount. Ideally, his intelligence merits a scholarship to higher education. He probably proceeds on to college and likely to post-graduate studies as well. He therewith finds himself among those of kindred interests and pursuits. Here he is able to speak to people on his level of communication and engagement, and he finds it enriching and inspiring. He probably also finds it influential in his selection of career. Is that career likely to be one that takes him back to his rural community, or is he more likely to remain among his intellectual kind? Plus, aside from just the intellectual compatibility issue there is the matter of cultural compatibility. With his rare and powerful intellectual capacity he is likely to seek pursuits in the more progressive realms of science and technology which are part and parcel the mode of the more advanced, industrialized cultures. Such cultures are likely to de-emphasize religious orientation as guideline to one's relationship to life and its meaning, as formerly was usually the case. A religious base is still with us, to be sure, but scientific thought, though relatively new in arrival to the human scene, has gained such prominence over the past five hundred years that it is now generally seen as the best hope for explaining man and his world. The Black race, collectively, is just emerging from the animistic, hunter-gatherer level of cultural organization and is moving on to the religious mode

57

of thought. With the help of a proselytizing White society it has leaped forth to monotheism though it still carries a strong strain of magical and theurical thinking as seen in Voodoo and other sorcerous practices. The Black level of cultural development thus seems to be in the early religious phase and perhaps that's why its leaders so often carry the honorific of "Reverend" though the theologic basis and societal purpose of such may be at significant variance from the White application of the term. Hence the Black man of unique intellectual endowment would be inclined to move into a cultural perspective more compatible with deployment of his talents, and that would be the Scientific-Industrial World. So not only does the Black Race have significantly fewer such members, but it loses them to more advanced cultures where their contributions not only would be better rewarded but also not shaded by Race, a boon as befits the dignity of Science as it should ideally and impartially be. The Black Race's leadership pool is thus not only reduced but its residual falls back on a lesser cultural style which inclines it to a compensatory use of political means for bridging the cultural gap.

But suppose the gifted Black man indeed decides upon politics as his pursuit. He then has a vast network of support awaiting him, some of it custodial and much of it tribal in nature, and perhaps with it even a crucially large White element motivated by lament over the Black man's long-standing lesser societal and economic status on the world stage. A White-based need to do exemplary national penance may also contribute to the simplistic notion that the Black man's current woes derive undeservedly from an earlier period of enslavement, thus encouraging also the Black man's popular understanding of his problem. This gifted Black man might readily draw upon such a rich and handy trove of motive, and his agenda would likely of necessity take the stamp of tribal reprisal and economic redress and so much less that of patriotic advocacy of the nation itself. Moreover, other nations holding grievances against this nation, whatever their basis, would be kindred to his purpose and likely his allies in policy (See Entry II). One can imagine that this

Black leader would see his agenda as achieving White parity for the Black citizens, even for the Black race in general so that the present societal, economic, and industrial gap can be closed.

But such a gap cannot be adequately addressed, much less erased, by economic and political preferment. Governmental expenditures may indeed open doors of opportunity for the Black man, and social programs may ameliorate some of the deleterious effects of lagging cultural development. Plus, humane and compassionate support by the more advanced cultures can only improve the societal lot of a lesser culture whose members, though skilled in hunter-gatherer ways more appropriate to primitive environments, find themselves unable to care for their own in an advanced Scientific-Industrial-Technologic society. And the problem cannot simply be legislated away. Nor can it be solved by political ideologies which ordain all citizens equal in material wealth. Punishing the winners, cultural and economic, for being successful does not offer incentive for future progress though it may assuage the envy and bitterness of the lesser world players. However, the Black man with superlative intellectual capacity just might then come to see, as likely would also his White and Oriental compatriots, the blessing of giftedness being ideologically and also categorically blunted thereby with the consequence that the potential beneficiaries of a free-ranging enterprise, beneficiaries such as himself as well as others, now perversely deprived of gain, and all in the name of equal opportunity, equal wealth, and equal society. Such an ideology might be imposed as a solution to the imbalance come of natural differences in endowment, individual as well as cultural, but it would be at the cost of personal freedom, the single most essential element for the progress of the human spirit. In effect, a more pervasive form of bondage offered, oddly, in the name of equality and freedom. And so, such an ideology might thus largely be a toilsome and oblique acknowledgment of the insolvability, by political means, of the natural evolution of innate individual and group differences, differences which simply cannot be fully effaced, and the ideology cited might thus more be, not actually a plan for societal progress, but merely a holding operation in the face of relentless natural selection governed by other forces. The gifted of our general kind just might see the struggle as not worth the effort. We would then have a distinct cultural failing. And it would be politically driven. Plus, it would offer no future other than that come of maintaining a status quo in which natural winners would not be able to pursue freely their creative potential and its rewards, while the natural losers would be protected from becoming even more distant also-rans. Though such an ideology carries a clear overall negativity, the losers might greet its mandated protection of them as a distinct benefit, short term and artificial though it be, for in the long run they would likely become even bigger losers, though with more company, as is usually the case in a stagnant and blighted society. See almost any Black sub-Sahara "nation." The effort would bespeak a distinct humanity of sorts, but it would not let Freedom ring.

05 September 2009

IX

Deprivation, Denial, Displacement

Discussion of the normal distribution of human intelligence raised the question of the Black man's innate disadvantage in a modern, technologic, industrial society, and it was also suggested that his accordingly limited store of Culture Capital offered him little remittance in view of that overriding disadvantage. In addition it was agreed that in I.Q. testing nurture played a significant but restricted rôle not only in test attitudes but also in test aptitude, though generous allowance for such in modified test design still resulted in durable Black-White score differences of significant magnitude. Moreover, it was held that such difference bore directly on the adaptation style as seen in the American Black man's relationship to the much larger White society of the nation. For example, the "poor" sector of our society is predominantly Black and is called so to avoid designation of socio-economic class specifically by race. Even if there are penniless recent arrivals from the Orient on hand they are not truly considered members of the "poor" class. Not even impoverished Whites, for that matter. No, the descriptive seems to apply distinctively to the Black poor. But why is that so when members of other racial groups or minorities may be equally poor but are somehow excluded from this genre to leave it preferably the realm of Blacks and designated so for referring exclusively to Black status in this country? The reason may have several facets. Firstly, it is a handy political device as might appeal to the compassionate side of the electorate, a potential benefit that probably would not come of referring to such Blacks as "the unsuccessful" or the "welfare recipient" class, and certainly not "the dysfunctional, socio-economically aberrant" class. To some degree those references also would aptly apply to the Black poor, perhaps less to the White poor, and likely not at all to the Oriental poor, and the reason seems to be based on the notion of recoverability. Many Whites slip into the Welfare Class during great depressions, and Orientals as well, but they usually don't stay there when opportunity comes for them to move forth. What we see in this particular is the vast difference between being "broke" and being "poor" and what it says about potential for recoverability, a perhaps seminal distinction derivative of Culture Capital. If so, such recoverability would not apply in equal degree to the Black members of the "Welfare Class," compared to other races, even when favored by Affirmative Action initiatives. Some do move on, for sure, but the Welfare Class remains predominantly Black and also disproportionately Black. Also true is the fact that some Blacks have indeed moved on to notable achievement in our society, even to commanding presence in science, commerce, academia, and government. Certainly this applies at least as well in the sports and entertainment worlds. So why is it that so many do not move on? It is no secret among themselves that the more gifted ones do tend to move on, whether their gifts are in the artistic, athletic, or intellectual fields, or blends of all three. So it is even among themselves that individual differences have much to say in regard to capacity for adapting and succeeding though all may have started out as "poor." Here again the rôle of innate givens seems crucial; material deprivation may be a common starting point for many but individual capacity may define quite different lifestyles and pursuits. And also results.

This assessment may apply on other levels of reference as well. The separate races likely started out at similar points of deprivation since we cannot imagine that nature personally favored one over another, given that they all likely started out in the same general region of the world, the prevailing theory holds. Or that nature was unfair in favoring one against another. The laws of natural selection might indeed be biased in favor of survival but they are applied equally to all species. And as we know, some species do well across the board while some do not. We also know that within a given species set the emergence of a more adaptive strain of that species is eventually followed by the extinction of the less adaptive strain of that set, such as in the Hominid family itself and specifically in the separate paths of the Neanderthal and Cro-Magnon species as a case in point. More on that later.

But our focus just now is the apparent intransigence of the Black Poor in the face of opportunity and encouragement for moving up in the socio-economic scale and why this intransigence is mirrored by the larger society's strong resistance to framing an answer more explanatory of and keeping with the minimal results come of policies vigorously fostered and implemented in the service of socially and politically tolerable answers which, though dissembling, readily lend themselves to a corrective activism, but regrettably an activism more conveniently pursued in the light, not in the dark where the actual problem may lie. So it appears our wont has been to define causes whose corrective address is well within the register of acceptable initiatives. Here again the distinction between cause and consequence is blurred and a certain collaboration is required of society and its needy sector to keep it so. At its best such collaboration can yield humane assistance and also support of the disadvantaged Poor with a certain lessening of their plight, particularly for those who have an innate capacity to redress deficits in their Cultural Capital. But such initiatives are aimed at the more malleable consequences of the problem, not the problem which generates those consequences in the first place. At its worst this practice mimics the pathos of a dog biting the stick thrown at him, not the thrower. But such is the nature of displacement: it avoids the distress, and perhaps the futility, a larger problem poses and then safely thrashes some secondary consequence of it to keep the basic problem conveniently unspoken.

So, judging by the results of our corrective initiatives for bringing the Black sector of our society up to socio-economic parity we have been looking for causes and their corrections in the more convenient, hopeful, and perhaps more humane light where accessible consequences abound. But it also appears we have agreed to stand good whatever cost may come of remaining safe from openly and collectively acknowledging the real problem, even to the point of erecting entire socio-political structures ostensibly dedicated to increasing the light, ironically. Thus the phenomenon that the more done in the name of good, the worse the problem gets. Ask any doting and desperate parent of an incorrigible child whose mal-adaptive behavior is inadvertently accommodated and reinforced by misdirected efforts at remedying it. The circumstance of good effort causing a worsening of the situation bespeaks a wretchedly wrong take on the problem and its cause. Such "good" effort put forth in the name of remediation is not unlike taking the consequences in our teeth and thrashing them about, over, and over, and over. But it makes for good political copy. More on that later. The basic prob-lem seems to be that there is a disconnect between the Black race and the White, Yellow, and perhaps even Red races. This disconnect is based upon the vast difference among the races in the level of their cultural development as demonstrated perhaps more clearly in this country where they live cheek by jowl. But we are reminded, as above, that many Blacks seem able, nonetheless, to bridge that cultural gap readily enough and with notable success. But the prob-lem is not with those successful individuals, but with the large majority of Blacks, the "poor," who continue to demonstrate that dis-connect; the very ones who make the disconnect identifiable by race. The White and the Yellow races are not identical, to be sure, but their levels of cultural development are similar. Both have their own written languages though the Yellow race till relatively recently relied on a pictographic, not phonetic, alphabet, the Korean alphabet excepted. Both have historical records of their societal efforts across time, including efforts at codified law. Both have an art beyond cere-monial enactment and one which is art for art's sake as a means of exploring man's relationship to his world. Both have gone beyond animism and hold deistic religions, the Whites foremost in this regard. And both have science in their record, again the Whites hold-ing the advantage in this pursuit. Yet foremost is the apparent ability of each race able to integrate useful and beneficial aspects of each other's cultures for enrichment of their own cultural store. The problem here is that the Black race has so little of its own culture to enrich. Sub-Sahara Africa is a case in point. It is surrounded by a world steeped in industry and technology but has shown little capacity for drawing upon such in updating its status among nations. The key seems to be that sub-Sahara Africa has, by dint of its impoverished culture and the multiple reasons for such, only a limited capacity for integrating and sustaining the benefits of White and Yellow achievements. Black Africa may be able to use wrist watches and computers but it may be a very long time before it can build any of its own, much less develop its own technology. It seems to be a given that if a culture has not over the course of its history developed its own written language, it's that much farther behind in developing a competing industry or technology.

It can be, and is said, that the arrival of the White man, and Yellow men as well, caused significant disruption of what existed of Black African culture. The social breakdown occasioned by slavery and imperialism can't be doubted, but the White man also brought the gifts of civilization as well. Yet there followed only modest enhancement or development of Black culture therewith. Plus, not all Blacks were made slaves, yet the benefits of civilization did not rapidly diffuse throughout Africa. Not even today with slavery and colonization long gone. Thus, much of Africa societally remains Africa as it was thousands of years before the White man came, and especially so where the White man has seldom trod.

The issue seems to be a given culture's capacity to access and grow. A parallel could be seen by the example of having an Alien group colonize the earth. The Aliens would possess unimaginable technology to have mastered interstellar travel, at least unimaginable to humans, and the Aliens would open Earth to a new dimension of existence. The human race would immediately become a subordinate life form both dependent upon and vulnerable to the Aliens' interests. Some human beings, those being five or six standard deviations to the right, might find themselves able to comprehend and access the technology and knowledge of the Aliens and find some place of participation among them, yet never possess their unique sapience for fitting in their "world," so to speak. But those superior human beings would be so few there would be very limited cross pollination to fellow human beings for the advancement of human culture compared to that of the Aliens. Yet human culture would forever be altered. Parity with the Aliens might come over time; but that span of time would likely be geologic in magnitude. Plus, Alien development would not come to a standstill in the meantime, waiting. Humans, as a race, would likely never catch up despite the great advances the Aliens would make available to them. A human mutant might appear to move the process along, but here again we are talking about many thousands of years. This did not happen between Neanderthal and Cro-Magnon despite an overlap of at least fifteen thousand years. But if the Aliens and the humans could inter-breed, the process would likely proceed more rapidly. However, it would ultimately and much sooner bring an end to the Human Race as it is and become something much different; to wit, a creole, and one more adaptive and progressive than the Human Race now is, but an inferior race still, compared to the Aliens.

The challenge to the Black race vis-à-vis the other races is just as cosmic. And the choices are just as wretched. And the outcome just as inevitable from the standpoint of race survival. It's the inevitability of the matter which bespeaks its tragedy so demanding of the salving defenses of denial and displacement.

And what say our leaders? Are they, cynical or unknowing, the bellwether practitioners of a dedicated denial and displacement? They're certainly thrashing about, don't we know, and not one of them is looking in the dark.

And what does this say about the essential, actual poverty of the "poor"?

11 September 2009

X

Evolution at its Worst

In the preceding entry the grim consequences come of a wholly unexpected Alien colonization of Earth were considered. The example was also offered as an amplified parallel to the White man's colonization of sub-Sahara Africa and other lands where the Black man is autochthonous. The consequent altered status of the Human race in the scenario of Alien visitation was likened to what the Black man experienced when White imperialism reached his lands. Mention was also made of the unbridgeable evolutionary gap which would separate the Human race from unimaginably advanced Aliens with the result that Human beings would necessarily become dependent and responsive co-inhabitors of the planet in a way not seen since Neanderthal and Cro-Magnon crossed paths some fifty thousand or so years ago with the gradual extinction of Neanderthal some fifteen thousand years later. According to what is known of the paleontologic record, Neanderthal's extinction proceeded slowly, perhaps helped along by violent confrontations, but in the main likely by the usual evolutionary process of a more adaptable and capable species simply replacing another.

Correspondingly it would be a consummate act of faith to believe that the Human race would endure in the face of Alien colonization. If the Alien intent is essentially benign or, better yet, even proselytic we Humans would still be able to go only so far in identifying with the Aliens because our level of intellectual development and the culture we use as scaffolding in our construction of life's meaning would likely carry us only so far in what we would be able to access of the Aliens' "world," so to speak. Human beings would forevermore have the role of also-rans and would likely fade away over time in the face of the Alien presence. The usual efforts at resurgence would be seen, but acts of belligerence and "nationalist" re-affirmation and such would amount to little. Evolution would have spoken, and life would obey. And Human beings daily would be reminded of such in that they would come to enjoy some of the benefits of a technology never before available to them and which would enrich and even facilitate their cultural growth, but growth as only their Human capacity could permit. There would also likely be spin-off groups which would resist such change and remove themselves from the mainstream in an effort to protect a certain cultural purity along with its founding heritage. There would likely also be reactionary "nationalist" movements to reclaim Earth as it had always been known. There might even be a call for a "fair" and leveling Socialism. But even if the Aliens were generously and benevolently tolerant of such resistance the ineluctability of natural selection would work its inexorable effect, and even if the Aliens made the effort to raise the Earthling above his previous level of cultural accomplishment, the net overall effect would be limited because of the Earthling's markedly limited innate capacity compared to that of the Aliens. After all, they found us; we didn't find them. As said, some five standard deviation Humans might grasp some level of Alien technology but they would be so few, and, too, they would be limited by a capacity nowhere near that of five standard deviation Aliens. These gifted Humans would hold the promise of the Human race but they would likely be only modest participants in the World's new future. In effect, they and their less gifted brethren would soon "top off" in accessing as much as they could of the Aliens' vastly richer technology and culture. Giving these Earthlings, with their limited capacity for comprehending cosmology, access to the arcania of such an advanced culture would be little better than providing someone who has great difficulty in reading and in understanding what he reads copies of one hundred of the world's greatest literary classics. There would be little to show for the effort, and similarly benighted humans would daily feel the frustration of being lesser than the Aliens and unchangeably so despite the efforts of each. That wretched state would soon result in the institution-alization of such salving blandishments as the claim of unequal schooling, material and wealth inequity, bias in opportunity, and the stunting effect of subjugation and durance. Even if the Aliens were compliant and "humane" enough to support measures for encourag-ing Human enrichment, such as grouping the young of the Earthlings and the Aliens together in shared schools, or extending to Human Beings preference in enlisting their participation in the new world, the result would be negligible for the Earthlings as a race since such preference would likely be accessed beneficially only by a capable few of them. It would likely settle into a matter of Earthlings, gifted or not, enjoying and profiting from the technologic marvels of the Alien race, yet themselves not at all able to generate such on their own, perhaps till well beyond some barely imaginable future. We Earthlings simply might not even be on the evolutionary track that could take us to such parity; ours might simply lead to an evolutionary dead end in the face of Alien superiority, just as happened to Neanderthal after a quarter of a million years of existence, yet fading away in the comparatively short overlap of fifteen thousand years shared with Cro-Magnon. Such is the nature of evolution and natural selection.

Given that such a view is based on a time frame of tens, even hundreds of thousand years one can yet note similar circumstances and their trends operating in a more immediate perspective. America is the most technologically and industrially advanced nation on Earth. The Black presence in America is the largest contingent of such in any fundamentally non–Black society. The cultural and societal dif-ferences between White and Black America were incomparably vast when the Black man was brought to these Alien shores and those differences remain even today after almost three hundred years of Black enculturation. It is also said that White America has assimi-lated more of Black America than Black America has assimilated of White though they have been equally exposed to each other and for exactly the same length of time. Here again capacity to assimilate offers telling differences. The usual reasons given for such invariably cite consequences, not causes, though they do sustain a measure of hope if seen as so. Thus their value. They also acquire political utility. Yet, it has also been said that legislated affirmation and preferment has worsened Black America's plight, and that well-intended measures, such as financial family subsidy, has undermined the rôle of the father in the Black home with the result that the black family has regressed to a more primitive, tribal level despite the best efforts on the part of all to have adaptation move forward, not backward.

It probably can be said that, all things considered and all self-serving cant put aside, the Black man in America, as a race, has at present "topped off." In view of the astounding enablements provided him over the past half century his relative, and, in some cases, his absolute status remains unchanged. It can also be speculated that his innate capacity has limited how much he can assimilate of what this society has offered with the result that, in effect, he can presently be only who he now is. Earthlings sharing this world with Aliens would know similar limitations and, in the face of the technological wealth the Aliens might make available to them, Earthlings would, by virtue of their limited capacity to assimilate generatively, remain fundamentally who they are and in no wise equal to the Aliens. And similarly, providing them with more and more of what they cannot developmentally use beyond servicing the necessities and comforts of modern life would amount to little more than to nourish a vengeful envy and a sense of entitlement come of feeling that something had been taken away from them, something like pride and self-respect. And this conviction certainly has a proven political utility but with no essential benefit to anyone, Black or White, save for race profiteers. And those are not at all in short supply.

"Salving blandishments." The term may provide portal to our appreciation of the personal, individual experience in this march of Destiny. We have used, as reference, terms such as "Race," "Alien," "geologic" and have employed a broad canvas of thousands of years and untold millions of individuals in collective portrayal of this theme. We have spoken in generic terms and have accordingly diluted the experience of the individual contributing his part to this drama. To do so makes such discussions more palatable and avoids a painfully pointed clarity of the individual's life this cosmic tragedy ordains.

Let's return to being Earthlings sharing the globe, more or less, with Aliens who are manifestly superior in culture and technology. Moreover, the Aliens which have landed on Earth, singular as they are, may not be from the top layer of the Aliens' science or industrial community, just like our airline pilots are not the theoreticians and aeronautical engineers who design their awesome aircraft. And let's say the average Earthling knows this. Worse, he knows his children know this. And he is too aware that he has brought forth children, as innocent as any can be, to live a life as inferior beings. The conflict between their knowing this—parents or children—and their striving not to know it imposes a sense of struggle to their existence which yet, by another reckoning, is at least *materially* improved by the Aliens' presence. But their sense of self and its value is not improved. In fact, it becomes a trade-off between personal dignity and material convenience. What would the Earthling father say to his children if they gauchely brought it up? For want of something better to offer would he merely abandon them to their fate? The Earthlings would know that the Aliens might prefer such lessers not be around at all but the Earthlings have no means to go anywhere else. They indeed now exist at the pleasure of the Aliens when previously they were the rulers of their own world, now a lost world. What would be their incentive to progress when their reach, now redefined by the Alien presence, would be so hopelessly beyond their grasp. Would the Earthlings work at making the best of it though never seeing themselves as more than a fated irredeemable lower caste resigned and compliant, or would they even bother at all, and renege totally on the drive to better the lot of their kind? Or would they cloak their remorse and distress in customary blandishments which, though tendentious and self-serving distortions, would lend a justice to their bitterness and orient their mood and energy toward establishing some kind of equality with the Aliens by whatever means necessary, though impossible such would be since the Aliens would remain the ones to sustain the advanced state of society and its improved conditions the Earthlings would otherwise not have and are now dependent upon, the forfeit of which would return the Earthlings to a less advanced state? This would be tantamount to Earthlings having reached their evolutionary dead-end along with their society. In effect, no matter what the benefit of their efforts to improve their general lot and no matter the promotion of their status, wherever the Earthlings stood in Earth's new society, they would stand no better than second, likely a very distant second. Perhaps Neanderthal could advise us well on this point. So also could social anthropologists.

It seems that the merest beginning of an approach to addressing a racial and social calamity would require specification of the problem as it really is and stop looking where the light is more convenient. A daring first step, yes, and one which, here in America, would depend upon concerned parties embracing compassion and courage, White compassion for the Black man's burden, and Black courage to see the burden for what it really is. Credit would be required both ways and from each to the other: the White man's courage to consider options long unacceptable to him but vital to the Black man's presence and compassion by the Black man for the White man's struggle in his mission to guarantee Life, Liberty, and the Pursuit of Happiness to *all* here in America. And just *maybe* . . . .

29 September 2009

XI

Wealth, Pleasure, Degeneracy

No one can doubt that America is the wealthiest nation the World has ever seen. Nor can it be doubted that American freedom, enterprise, and energy, exploited in the keep of a blessedly bountiful land, are what made it so. Nor can it be questioned that no other nation, ever, yielded such global power and exercised it so benignly, generously, and even protectively. With this as its résumé how can we understand the demand of some, with the covert compliance of many, that this nation abandon its exceptionalism and take a place among the lesser nations of the world, a sort of regression to the mean?

The usual answers offered indict political activism as the engine of such a regressive agenda. Class envy is usually seen as the source of passion fueling that engine, the blandishments of "social justice and equality" and "equitable distribution of wealth" notwithstanding. Such notions, claiming a quasi-historical legitimacy come of political exertions of various eras, have never realized a condition as successful as intended, but uniformly much less so, and certainly not as productive of a commonweal as is the bounty of American exceptionalism. Such activist agendas are usually pursued by lesser nations which have so much less to lose by such policies and indeed may have reason to expect significant material gain for the effort. Such expectancy carries the stamp of what could be called a "lifeboat mentality." Affected nations usually have significant urgencies not being addressed by their social and political milieu which ideally *should* allow and support the individual's God-given right to what we Americans recognize as Life, Liberty, and the pursuit of Happiness, but which, rather, attempts to manage a condition in which such freedom either is not allowed to take root or is not trusted. Such countries and their citizens have never known freedom on the scale Americans have long enjoyed it, either in the national or in the individual dimension. In this regard, these other nations are poor in precisely the way America is wealthy, and the difference in material dividends issuing from this distinction makes the contrast too emphatically clear: Americans have a veritable cornucopia of return to show for their ideologic wealth whereas nations not so enterprising or free are obliged to ration what becomes available to them, locked as they are in their regimented conception of life and its managed promise. Crowded into such a lifeboat, as it is suggested these citizens are, it would be unconscionable, they undoubtedly would think, that the good fisherman, though equally harnessed to the limited dimensions of the lifeboat, be allowed to keep all his catch while the poor fisherman be allowed to perish when all hands aboard are expected to man the oars jointly in hope of arriving at some better place. The previous entry details the larger cosmology of this point.

America has long been that bountiful and better place, and the oceans of difference which surround it to this day stand as challenges to those who are willing to parlay freedom with individual enterprise in pursuit of what Americans have long enjoyed. Some do, but so many others either will not, or cannot, and thus remain in their lifeboat to nowhere, perhaps hopefully guided by their ideologic stars but humbly unable to reach even the moon. That would require a measure of exceptionalism.

Most nations, by American reckoning, are rather poor, many squalidly so. And most nations are struggling to maintain a respectable and creditable position in the global lineup. Contenders for the pole position, long belonging to America, come and go as America races along. Americans enjoy the spoils of victory on a scale only imagined by other peoples of the world and the gap separating the rest of the world from American ascendency is seemingly unbridgeable. The scope of this gap is seen in the fact that just one of the fifty states of our Union has the seventh largest economy of the World. Just one!

Hence, America is categorically the gold standard of freedom, national wealth, enterprise, and productivity. The other nations of the World are bound to this point of reference, however regarded, and cannot avoid it in defining their own status and national prospects. Understandably some nations might prefer America not to be around at all because of what its presence tells them of themselves. Better, perhaps, that America be more like them to dispel any wretched contrast since they themselves must abandon any hope of themselves actually becoming equal to America, or better. It all hinges, it seems, on how you define your national identity, and redefining America collectively would thus seem globally kinder and more sensitive. Or so it is wished. More to come on that point.

But for the nonce let's put the rest of the World and its lifeboats aside and focus just on this nation, using the same lens of scrutiny. Let's say that though America holds the prospect of full and plenty for all of its citizens, there are yet those citizens who simply are unable to provide for themselves on the scale of the average American. Yet these less providential persons may actually live on a scale which would place them in the privileged class in some lesser nations. Though a matter of relativity and likely covertly understood to be so—the underprivileged of this nation seldom leave these shores to seek their fortunes elsewhere; quite the contrary—does this understanding lessen their grievance of having to do with less than, say, the better fishermen? Apparently not, since there is always present to some degree their embittered call for some to have less so that some can have more. The less privileged maintain the lament of being expected to row though receiving less for their effort. Thus, this nation's premise is at grim variance with the zero sum cast of such Lifeboat mentality. But since these persons are adrift, going nowhere, their plight argues that *any* change would be for the better. These citizens supply the ranks of an aggressive and resentful activism.

But as we suggested earlier, many more are covertly compliant in the face of activist rhetoric. Why so, if the compliant enjoy a blessed Providence matched nowhere else? Assuredly, if the under-privileged of this nation, as relatively well-provisioned as they are, see themselves as impoverished, though ardently envied by so many other people of the World, then one may assume that the average American working at his dream must see the better fishermen of the community as enjoying what also could, he may actually think, be rightfully his own even though what he already has is the envy of the World. His envy, it seems, continues exponential while his benefits remain linear. Most of these persons well recognize their view as being no less driven by their very *own* greed—a fruitless greed—and hence are not inclined to be fully open in their censure of the supposed same greed motivating the better fishermen. Hence, they tend to serve more as silent enablers of the more openly aggressive activists. And they help vote activist representatives to office.

But for the most part, most Americans are grateful for their lot and do see it as a product of this nation's blessing and its founding wisdom. And they have been comfortable in its blessing, secure in its wisdom, and protected in its compassionate reach. Pleasure is realized in its availability and variety as nowhere else, and the lion's share of it is available to even the average American. The result is that America's children often know nothing less than the doting liberality of their parents in a generously comfortable traverse of their youthful years, whose liberality now often extends well into adulthood. Just about every American can experience a relatively unencumbered adolescence, formerly the province only of the nobility in the rest of the World. For much of the rest of the World, the other industrialized nations exempted, only a basic minimum of schooling precedes one's entry into the workforce, and this is accepted as an economic necessity. Nowadays adolescence in America has been redefined to extend well into one's mid-twenties and is given over to pursuits loosely regarded as preparatory for suiting one to the waiting workforce. These pursuits have come to be seen by the individual adolescent as an entitlement, by the parents as a responsibility, and by the rest of the World a rank indulgence. These years accommodate a range of pleasures often never known to the parents themselves but which now command prevailing position not only both in the adolescent's expectancy but in the American mercantile scene as well.

Yet, it is, of course, all relative. The pleasures of one era, or culture, suit that setting while the pleasures of today, derivative of our current wealth, accordingly suit our current taste and expectancies. But, more to our point, do those differences now portend a countervailing and penalizing inevitability? Many think so, and, even more to the point, do those differences herald a national degeneracy come of a false Elysium?

Some have even studied the matter. Alexander Tytler, a Scottish lawyer and professor of History at the University of Edinburgh, published in the 1770's writings contemporaneous with our Declaration of Independence. He had made a study of the various Democracies known to history. His studies revealed that Democracies, as a rule, lasted about two hundred years and that they had in common certain stages in their growth and decline. Loosely, those stages begin with drums and flags and end with complacency and apathy and ultimately with loss of the democratic principle of government.

The stages noted by Tytler are:

> From bondage to spiritual faith
> From spiritual faith to great courage;
> From courage to liberty;
> From liberty to abundance;
> From abundance to complacency;
> From complacency to apathy;
> From apathy to dependence;
> From dependency back to bondage.

We might say that we're at the Complacency-Apathy-Dependency stage of the sequence in our national history, and signs of such abound, the major one of which is departure from our founding principles with increasing dependence upon central government to supply civic initiative and direction. In a word, transfer of power from the people to the governmental process in exploitation of the political vacuum come of the popular drift into a self-serving and self-focused complacency. Accordingly, there is an attendant and resultant apathy as to popular responsibility in sustaining a national credo.

It is at such times that the restive and resentful sector of our society, long aggrieved of their lesser station, see an opportunity to assert their demand for that which they could never realize by way of individual enterprise of their own. They thus turn to the governmental process made available to them by way of the larger populace's relaxation of responsibility in favor of contentment and apathy. Here again, examples, very current ones, abound.

This drift is proclaimed by its advocates as "progressive." Others see it as part and parcel the bellwether of national degeneracy. Its advocates see the aggrandizement of the less accomplished at the expense of the more successful as social and economic Justice; others see it as a corruption of the driving force of this nation, the driving force which creates the very wealth of the nation itself. The decision may lie with the peripherals, those dysgenic elements of our society to which we more lately have become accustomed.

There are certain peripherals which speak loudly of degeneracy. These peripherals are merely symptomatic, but, like all symptoms, contribute in feedback fashion to the velocity of the malady itself. Plus, these symptoms appear to be unassailable in their larger import. They are as follows:

1. *The Mexican Economy.* The drug trade contributes untold billions of American dollars annually to the Mexican economy. The actual amount cannot be known because of the contraband nature of it and its dependence on smuggling for its distribution. Moreover, it provides untold

numbers of home jobs to Mexicans who would otherwise be without work or else here in the illegal alien traffic as cheap labor. In any event, the alien workers here forward additional millions back to Mexico for family benefit. Perforce, what has to be seen as a conspiracy between the Mexican and American governments for the violation of their own laws, the criminal practice flourishes. But the burden of responsibility falls on this side of the Rio Grande. The American people want their drugs, business wants its cheap labor, Congress is recruited to the purchase of more votes, valid or otherwise, and the White House, seems to be as hooked as any of the other socio-political partakers in this mega-addiction. In a word, a large sector of our society and political process has become dependent on what the society and our political structure declare to be statutorily wrong and morally corrupt. But, as with all addictions, gratification comes first and consequences be damned. Plus, addicts say they can break their habit whenever they want, don't they? Notice that our government is careful not to ban outright the tobacco and liquor businesses. Such would result in too great a loss of revenue. Yet, the government is ardently in favor of good health, just as it is in favor of safe driving. A wise Russian fisherman once said that a fish rots from the head first.

2. *Obesity.* Americans are among the fattest people in the world. Several other smaller nations are recognized as contenders, but the sheer mass of American adiposity places this nation in the benchmark position. Here again the combined effect of Contentment, Apathy, and Dependency trace out their visible dietary effects. Few other nations have generated such a bloated industry in weight reduction diets and fitness programs, neither of which is any more effective than the Border Patrol is allowed to be.

Most people come out boldly in favor of good health, but their practices speak more emphatically of a commitment to ease and satiation. The colossal web of fast-food enterprises seems unable to satisfy the American appetite fast enough. Approximately half of Americans are diagnostically regarded as obese, and all of them are familiar with the deleterious effects obesity has on health. Very few books are written on the joys of morbid obesity. Yet, here again, immediate satisfaction rules. And besides, there is implicit faith in the surpassing skill of American medicine to fix anything that goes wrong, as it very often can in its unintended rôle of enabler.

3. *NEA.* The National Education Association, also known as the Teacher's Union, is offered as the third major sign of national degeneracy. It's membership has not only elected to withdraw from profession status, but has chosen to identify itself with union goals and tactics, plus the political affiliations which go hand and glove with such. We are all aware of the trickledown effect this has on the classroom. Formal education has lost more than a bit of its priority and curriculum now too often borders on indoctrination of trendy social and political ideology. Craft in teaching is now subordinated to the satisfaction of national quotas and social correctives and thus are biddably available to other, tactically collaborative agendas. A profession puts it ethic first and the life style of its membership follows accordingly. Benefits and emoluments to the membership follow secondarily. With a trade union, benefits come first and the craft's ethic, if any, is secondary and usually more anecdotal. Union organization confers power on its membership for bargaining purposes in securing benefits and preferments, and ethic is not part of the process. The NEA embraces such methods. Teacher strikes

are routinely called shortly before the beginning of the academic year, never at the beginning of the summer vacation. Thus the children and their schooling are held hostage. Wages and benefits are always the issue and protection of ethic and its supporting principles and practices are never in evidence. The result is that the NEA is amenable to just about any passing classroom fad or social initiative, and especially so to any profitable *political* or partisan recruitment. The results are as we see them: our teachers are comparatively the highest paid in all the industrialized nations of the world and our children rank lowest among those nations in academic achievement. And the NEA remains remarkably silent on the matter.

A contrasting perspective may be seen in the Dental Profession. Years ago the fluoridation of municipal drinking water became an issue of hot debate, and as usual, saw the typical line-up of knows and knows nots. The Dental Profession knew that fluoridations would lower the incidence of dental cavities; the knows nots, a collection of simple obstructionists and the-sky-is-falling quakebuttockses, fiercely opposed it. The dental Profession campaigned loud, clear, and energetically in favor of fluoridation knowing that if effected it would reduce their business and also their income. But they put their ethic and the general public's benefit first. And the result is before us: the frequency of dental cavities is markedly reduced and Americans have the finest dental health and care in the entire world. That's a profession in the finest meaning of its calling: the moral duty to be so effective as to put itself out of business. Moreover, its ethic is not a commodity for sale to the highest political bidder and therefore does not subordinate its practice to the tactics and goals some political agendas require, as does the NEA. Dentists remain their own persons—ethical—and they do not see their calling as a profession in name only. Nor does anyone else. Oddly, the rank

81

and file teachers do not in the least mind that they have the very finest dental care. After all, they are a *union*!

11 October 2009

XII

Envy, Despair, Hatred

In an earlier entry the unavoidability of individual differences was cited. It was also noted that such differences will likely pursue a curve of distribution for the more measurable ones, such as height or weight, and that this curve would carry predictive value. Also, to the extent the sample trait is randomized and of a sufficiently large population, its curve would likely trace a normal curve of distribution. Indeed, it is also known that while some measurable traits are modifiable, such as weight, some are not, such as height, and it is these fixed traits which bedevil remediation programs. True, the *sequelae* of such traits are often readily responsive to a remediation effort, but, even so, a tendency to revert to a more spontaneous, unfettered expression is ever present. Weight is a good example. A large sample of obese people can be put on controlled diets and we would soon see individual weight as well as group mean weight change favorably. But unless the controlled diet is enforced over time, the obesity usually returns to something of an individual "set point" which derives of habitus, life style, and general attitude, themselves measurable in their variations. For the favorable weight to be sustained the notion of enforcement assumes prominence. But such is nothing new to the human scene. Most aspects of membership in society carry a note of enforcement of obedience to the requirements of good standing, be it by way of vocation, family style, personal relationships, and even duties to oneself. The balance between accedence and personal freedom is usually a carefully calibrated one.

And so it is with the more societal sequelae of individual differences, sequelae such as wealth, status, dominance, and so forth. To regard such differences as mere happenstance, or the fell results of an unbridled societal unfairness, is not only categorical but also simplistic. Such conditions derive of a certain industry come of energy channeled by individual differences in the use of resources available to all. Molecules are present for everybody's use, but it is usually those who have a knack for using them in some gainful way who achieve distinction, and sometimes wealth, for making some beneficial product available to themselves and to the community. These persons can be chemists, distillers, even bottlers. They bring forth something novel for the public's consideration. These innovators may join together as teams, as in a company with all its layers of administration and production, but the essential ingredient in this construction is the individual aptitude for working with those bountiful molecules.

But such aptitude never exists in isolation within its possessor. Its influence in the make-up of the possessor's psyche often inclines toward other predilections as well. The chemist might have a knack also for cooking, the point being that individual aptitudes have a ripple effect across the possessor's persona such that a certain inevitable uniqueness is innate in all of us, given the multiplicity of our givens both in quantity and in quality. The only thing we all have in common is that we're all unique, like our fingerprints, though we all have fingers that look fairly much alike.

And we all have footprints, too. Despite large similarities in lifestyle—so many of us really like football—individual differences abound within the scope of generic interests. No two people witness the game, much less the individual players' performances, in the same way. Most can agree on the final score, but the individual experience of the game is another thing entirely.

The same applies to the game of life. We all play it, and the individual experience is unique for each player. And, yes, some of us rack up higher scores than others in any given meeting. And just as there are bad losers, there are also bad winners right along with the good losers and the good winners. Their individual experience tends to shine through, though all, more or less, agree to, and do, observe the *rules*. Fairness is certainly *intended* in that sense because the rules in the American Game of Life are no longer egregiously biased or prejudiced, but still indeed define winners and losers fairly. But if such fairness and its natural sequelae cannot be permitted, then the game ceases to be a game, *qua* game, and becomes a tedious communal exercise of dubious purpose and little attraction.

If people are so given to live their lives according to their natural, innate givens, plus those givens are individually variable with the result that a corresponding variability in individual benefit yield is inevitable *sui generis,* what is to be said of the difference in bounty come to each individual? More to the point, to whom does it belong? Let's say I'm five feet tall and my male peers are approximately six feet tall (that curve of distribution again). Also, let's say the average female is five and a half feet tall. Let's then say that those normally distributed women uniformly prefer men taller than themselves if for no other reason than that such an arrangement offers the women a larger sartorial palette, such as high heels, etc., though we know it goes far beyond that. And let's say I (RMC) want a tall, svelte, stylish woman just like my male peers have. But there are no takers, even though I am a productive, perhaps even romantic, law-abiding citizen. My only female respondents are about my size and not at all to my relish. Do I accept my unhappy lot and make the best of it, or do I seek kindred others to join with me in rising up to force social policy to over-ride natural predilection and have a tall girl of my choosing be forced to accept my suit though it would likely result only in our sharing a mutual disaffection? After all, though I would now have a tall girl I would also know she didn't truly want to be with me, but would prefer a tall mate and would be so much more satisfied alongside him. It would not be a happy arrangement for me or my tall girl—she wouldn't want to be with me and I would resent that she would prefer to be with a tall man. My envy of tall men would be stoked into jealousy and such would now be the backdrop of the relationship I had with my tall girl. Earlier, before our forced union, it was only I who was unhappy. Now, my mate, who could have been happy with a tall man, is as unhappy as I, if not moreso. Thus, our forced arrangement has not brought forth a shared happiness, but has made us about equally unhappy, with my jealousy now thrown in to boot.

Could such a thing be brought to pass? It would all depend upon the intensity of my envy and how much it is shared by others of my plight. If my envy over-rode my sense of another person's right to live his or her own fortunes freely, it assuredly might, simply because my short-comings, literally so in this sense, have prevented my acquiring naturally that which I covet. Restricting the freedom of others, though I have the self-same freedom but am unable to gain as much profit from it, would require of me a perspective which over-rides the individual's right to apportion his—or her—bounty as wished. And could this ever be countenanced, especially if the obligated and restricted individual resents the personal unfairness of it; that tall girl, for example?

Not only can it be countenanced, but it can also become a mission. If so, how could it recruit and gain impetus?. The simple, though not the full answer, is *bounty*, as mentioned. As long as a commonweal is poor, or relatively so, and scratching out a living is everybody's lot, there is not much to envy, one of the other. But let opportunity take root, and let it be extended by the availability of resources. Then mix such resources with industrialization, top it off with technology, and then let individual capacity exploit such op-portunity. The results, as well as their differences, become much more manifest, individually, nationally, and also internationally. Individual differences are played out on an ever-enlarging canvas, and great winners are rewarded as great losers are lamented.

This process, left to its own devices, would see an ever-widening gap between the winners and the losers though even the losers would profit from the trickledown effect of an enriched commonweal. Yet, though my material comfort is enlarged accord-ingly, I'm still only five feet tall and the six foot men continue to get what I want. It's the difference that counts and it won't go away, no matter how improved my lot. If anything, my improved lot may carry a note of futility that things will never change in my direction, no matter how hard I or anyone else works to contribute to the commonweal's enrichment. Despair awaits. My improved lot begins to feel like a sop, a bribe, to sustain acceptance and compliance as I continue to work on in my deprived state.

But soon the day will come that I'll tire both of my compliance and of my frustrated state, and I'll come to see the successful beneficiaries of society as wicked profiteers. Plus, others of my lot may now be making restive sounds as despair looms ever closer for them, too, since there are a lot of other malcontents who are figuratively only five feet tall, don't we know. Resistance to despair mobilizes a militancy because the time has come for resistance, not acquiescence. Externalizing the problem by projecting on to the successful beneficiaries a gross unfairness of purpose—purpose contrived of hoarding the better things in life, the better things *all* should have—soon becomes the tactic key to underwriting the militancy. And it also provides a rallying cry for firing up activist morale . Strategies and tactics now begin to take shape and their tariff requires that the concept of fair play be skewed beyond recognition to fit what has now become a push for power. The more successful and productive the industrial-technologic society becomes in rewarding winners and defining losers, the more "unfair" it is seen to be. In the meantime, just about all of those successful five foot six girls are still teaming up with those successful six foot men and having a grand time of it. It's an outrage that can be corrected only by an enforced "fairer" distribution of societal resources so that the short people can be served more favorably. Of necessity all are now less-free citizens and are more mere commodities for distribution in accordance with the doctrine of not only sharing the wealth but also being shared along with it. The cost of such an enterprise would of course thus come at the expense of personal freedom which now would be seen doctrinally and necessarily as an aberration too often leading to a regrettable and selfish independence. Alas, but we would now all be *equally* un-free, wouldn't we be? And the sharing of that baleful condition would be offered as balm to the troubled soul and to the store of capitalized hatred now common to all, it would be hoped, for then we could doctrinally as well as socially ignore unwanted individual differences even if they refuse to go away. It would be simply a matter of knowing which eye to keep closed, even at the cost of societal depth perception.

The upshot? All would be locked in a morbid, collective degeneracy in which each holds the other responsible for what life has become. The recognition of futility, come of loss of the very freedom which might sustain hope of a better day, hastens that futility along to its inevitable devolution into Hatred—hatred of life, its content, and of what it now came to mean; something less than the hopeful Pursuit of Happiness so wisely solicited by our Founders. Class hatred would successfully be changed into a collective hatred of life, but life would now be seen as more "fair."

09 November 2009

XIII

American Politics: The Art of the Impossible

We have already noted that the Demographics of America are like nowhere else on this planet. The mix of races, cultures, and their histories is extensive and rich enough to confound all innocent and generous attempts to fathom and explain the swirling social, political, and economic currents generated of the populace's energies spent in the pursuit of Happiness, a quest which hosts an ever-copious variety of uncertainties along with personal predilections. The guarantee and protection of Life, once an American given, has lately been cast into debate even over the rights of the unborn living, while Liberty, formerly an estate universally venerated and proclaimed as God-intended, is the very one which keeps the currents of daily living restive and threatening. Liberty threatening? Apparently so, for only in its splendid isolation as a universal does it seem divinely benign. But "only" suggests innate, imposed limitations and restrictions at play in the very condition dedicated to the freedom from such. How can this be?

The notion of "splendid isolation" seems to be key to the matter. Can anything actually claim "splendid isolation"? We presume so simply by dint of our being able to conceive of such a state, if we actually can. But even so, the notion seems to beg the condition of such a "splendor" being recognized by a not so splendidly isolated accompaniment generic to the very perception of it. Or, to say it another way, liberty applied to what? The notion of its having a referrant places a condition on its isolation, and what kind of isolation is that? And what could be splendid about it?

The issue is not mere semantics. This has to do with Universals and the inevitable departure from them we experience when we undertake to apply them in defining our reality by dint of the principles we select for its management.

It might be possible for one single person—totally isolated—to experience Liberty in closest approach to its true essence. He could go as he wished and to where he wished. Or not. He could sleep when he wished, where he wished, and for as long as he wished. Again, or not. This liberty of action could apply to all aspects of his embrace of his perceived reality. He would draw upon the essential liberty inhering in every dimension of his isolated world, isolated by the very "solitarity" of his own existence. Being a hermit, à la remontado, could thus well be seen as the pursuit of splendor.

But true success in that pursuit would likely soon enough cancel his status as a living, mortal aspirant. Moreover, even if he were partially successful in his pursuit, what about the world around him and its assorted beings responding to the similar promise of Liberty's reach? The fauna and flora also draw upon a waiting splendor very much as each has its own existence defined. Thus, if our aspirant eats a carrot or catches a fish he is exercising a bondage on other life at the great expense of their liberty. Could there then be competing liberties, each capable of invading that of the other? Not likely. The animistic Environmentalists stand ever-ready to elaborate on this point.

So maybe when we talk of having and enjoying Liberty we are not talking about Liberty at all, but about something else loosely identified as Liberty. And maybe the presumer to an essential and splendid Liberty must needs be as isolated in his quest as Liberty is in its meaning.

But none of us is so isolated. Indeed, we're rather crowded together collecting the benefits of our group and individual social contracts. And, for the most part, respecting each other's rights. We can no longer come and go exactly as we please, or how. Rather, we have to drive on the right side of the road, at least still so in this country, and stop when the traffic light tells us to. We can't go to work whenever the spirit moves us—that is, if our sustenance is not totally of our own doing. Were it so, our life style would be more feral in its isolation. So, living among our peers bespeaks a compromise traditionally known as the social contract: we forfeit some things to gain others, and some of those "others" are held to be important to Life and Happiness. But Liberty, as we have defined it, is now nowhere to be found. What do we have left in its place? We have *Freedom*, in varying negotiated degrees.

For example, it is constituted that we Americans have the right of free speech, but yet we could not use that right to exempt ourselves from the penal consequences of shouting "Fire!" in a crowded movie theatre, as so often is noted. To shout so would be exercising the right of free speech, to be sure, but the result would be a violation of the other moviegoers' right to Life and the protection of it. The same may be said of our other mandated rights.

The issue then seems to be the difference between Liberty as a metaphysical construct and Freedom as a political proposition. Liberty, like Circularity and Wednesdays, may indeed exist, but not in our actual world, though circles and days do. This perhaps may explain why leaders of the most cruel and oppressive regimes may hail Liberty as their gift to their subjects, but never mention the word Freedom. Would be just too great a gaffe, that.

And just what does this ontologic disquisition have to do with anything beyond a classroom exercise? Simply, it can be shown to have significant say-so in our courtship of the current political virtue of social Diversity.

We all know that "Diversity" is a political device to render more palatable the blatant wrongs of Affirmative Action, such wrongs violating as they do the principles of fair play and equality under the law (See Entries I and VI), the very basic givens of social commerce between citizens as defined by our founding charter. The fairness principle deals with honoring agreed-upon covenants in our dealings with each other, and the equality principal is the vehicle by which fairness gains its traction. Thus, favoring some over more qualified others as an attempt at correcting fundamental and transcendent differences, or social imbalances, even historical ones, constitutes a wide departure from the proposed purpose of our founding charter with the result that our freedoms, and the preservation of such, are placed second to political and social expedience. "Diversity," while offered as an emollient to an Affirmative Action agenda so chafing to citizens following the hard, straight pathway, is actually an aggravant to the very condition it undertakes to soothe. For example, Diversity is taken to include the notion of heterogeneity. It is a given that if everybody were socially and culturally the same, there would be no Diversity; the rules and laws of the group would favor all equally. But to have Diversity, differences have to be protected, even encouraged, to justify adjustment of those rules, and certainly for enactment of laws needed to sustain such adjustments. But such adjustments may run counter to the social and cultural practices of others with the result that an intercultural-social polemic is created. In an extreme example, doctrinal debate is given to the "rights" even of illegal aliens. These aliens are violating the nation's laws by being here illegally, and are thus by law disqualified as bona fide *legal* citizens upon whom this nation's governance and mandates bestow carefully defined rights and privileges. Yet the aliens are at discussion as to what rights and privileges might *unlawfully* be granted them by our government. To a lesser degree, the same applies to some groups *legally* here on this soil preserving and practicing their cultural and social uniqueness, such as in subcultures. This in itself need not be an assault on the freedom of others, but as soon as those predilections and practices are underwritten by laws obliging all others to a special obedience then Diversity comes at the expense of equal Freedom. For example, we might not be able to mail a letter on a certain day because to keep the Post Office open for such might offend another. At least one of us has to lose something. Or, hiring an illegal alien or a less qualified legal citizen in a competitive market and, in the latter case, being required to do so by law does indeed constitute an assault on the freedom of others. Such an assault is imposed in the name of

Diversity, and the general citizenry is required to embrace such as a favorable trade-off. Our government has now, largely, appointed itself as barterer of our Freedom rather than protector of it. Regrettably, the result of such enterprise can never be more ennobling or uplifting than are the motives of the barterers. Our legislators may have lost their way, but in their vagrancy they have awarded us commendably Diverse restrictions of our Freedom in the very same breath they speak of Liberty for all. One wonders if they even bother to notice.

11 November 2009

XIV

President Strangelove

Most Americans are familiar with the 1960's movie, *Doctor Strangelove*, in which a psychotic Air Force General unilaterally undertakes to inflict nuclear punishment on the Soviet Union for its threats to America's "precious bodily fluids." No one knew the General to be psychotic until an incident occurred which negated the General's usual control in suppressing his delusional thinking from view. Once in the open, like a *bête noir* out of its cage, his delusion took over his psychic function and his behavior followed accordingly. During his psychotic decompensation the General was obsessed with protecting "our precious bodily fluids," saw it as a Messianic mission, knew that he was ordained to fulfill that mission, was dismissive of any logic to the contrary and cared not a wit about the massive destruction to come of his protection of those precious bodily fluids. Such is the nature of fixed delusions; they orient the function and faculties of the mind around the absolute necessity of fulfilling the demands of the delusion, often anointing the subject's self in identification with the Divine, such as a Second coming, or, more personalized, in the rôle of a Savior entitled to all the powers necessary for the fulfillment of his mission. To him his rôle and his mission are beyond question, and they are proof to all logic and reality brought to bear by concerned others who often are thwarted by the Psychotic's loyal following of like-thinking retainers who may not be as delusional as he but who are keen to exploit the Psychotic's mission in satisfaction of their own agendas. Recent historical figures leap to mind; the human predicament has never been shy of saints and sinners, and psychotic ones at that. Indeed, the grandiose Messiah of psychotic thinking is the representative of the nether side of religion—all religions—and his disciples typically play the rôle of

95

liaison with the sane world, the very world the psychotic Messiah undertakes to change or even destroy.

That's the usual pedigree of Paranoia. It's etiologic, basal relationship to a blighted sexuality is considered and pursued elsewhere and is not germane to our present discussion though traces of such an element may be detected in the milieu the Paranoid constructs for himself, the dynamic meaning of which is also totally lost upon him but quite correctly captured in "Doctor Strangelove" in that the very first time our psychotic General consciously realized his ordained mission to protect and preserve our precious bodily fluids was while he was in the act of making love, perhaps too much an unguarded and enabling moment for him and his organizing delusion to resist.

The world of Politics, perhaps currently more often than does the world of Religion, provides us with a view on this phenomenon, and perhaps also the more destructive side of it, though Religion is not shy of world cataclysm mounted in the name of Faith. But, for the most part, Politics usually has the more available and ready armamentarium for the prosecution of its campaigns. And we all know that when Politics and Religion are allied in some crusade the destruction can be extreme because, here again, sanity is too often subordinated to salvation, of all things.

As suggested above, the Paranoid Messiah usually has ample disciples gathered around him. Often those disciples are fanatical in their devotion to him. Their rôle, as suggested, is to function as liaison with the sane, usually infidel world, and they function, apostle-like, in carrying the Messiah's message and also prosecuting his reforms. Though often fanatical they usually are not so totally given to delusion as to see themselves a Messiah as well; the world usually can only afford one of those at a time. Hence their reality ties, though seriously attenuated, are capable of serving as the linkage for their liaison function to have its effect. This arrangement sees its less pathologic form in standard gatherings such as Boards, Councils, Panels, and even Cabinets, any one of which can be as diseased as the worst.

Last week an unspeakable tragedy occurred at one of our domestic military installations, a mere few days after Veterans Day when we annually honor the fallen of our Armed Forces. President Obama observed the ritual of the Commander in Chief placing a wreath on the monument honoring those who fell in defense of our Freedom. It was just a few days later a homicidal fanatic, a Muslim terrorist, himself a member of our military but with covert ties to Jihadists abroad, opened fire on his defenseless fellow American soldiers, killing thirteen and wounding thirty more. He himself was wounded and then rushed to hospital for emergency care. It was an unprovoked attack, except by way of current international initiatives by our military to which the shooter took offense. Moreover, he had given repeated and impassioned warning to all levels of his social and professional peer group as to his mounting frenzy and belligerence. Regrettably, his supervisors and his superiors, fully informed of his deviant behavior, felt paralyzed by Political Correctness such that their fear of appearing "intolerant" over-rode common sense and responsible judgment. Even today some of them continue to see their dutiful malfeasance as defensible in their pursuit of approval by and obedience to a higher, overseeing authority. One wonders who they believe the enemy actually to be. They will of course remind us that they were simply obeying orders, the traditional haven of military criminality.

President Obama, plus the entire nation, felt it meet that he publicly address the tragedy and provide a measure of guidance in the horror and grief felt by all. He called a news conference and his un-scripted address was carried on all the major TV networks. We were all prepared to be led in dole and to have our resolve affirmed. However, President Obama opened his address with a two-minute preachment on the historical and continuing abuse inflicted on Native Americans by an evil White government. He spoke of treaties being broken, lands stolen, and campaigns of annihilation mounted against the Native Americans who resisted. The message was clear: abused people have the right, even duty, to rise up against their abusers.

He then, and only then, proceeded to speak of the tragic shootings. He used the proper words in decrying the carnage, careful to avoid addressing it as another terrorist attack on Americans on their own soil. He continued the official policy of not accounting the escalating warning signals provided by the gunman who was preferably seen as a lone malcontent who had reached some kind of a breaking point. The shooter's avowed membership in and active advocacy of a terrorist movement which the United States military is currently undertaking to defeat on the field of battle was quickly discounted. Yet President Obama, in his two-minute preamble, had made it clear that people have the moral right to oppose their abusers, then as now. It set a tone for the rest of his delivery which, in a way one could perhaps see as an allusion to certain chickens having "come home to roost" to beteem the dead and wounded for their being agents of abuse, especially of those people dear to the shooter.

We think we have before us a regrettable demonstration of what is sometimes called "leakage" symptoms: behavior, either verbal or physical, which leaks out—breaks forth—beyond the restraints imposed by the sufferer's caution, judgment, conscious suppression. We say "sufferer" because this phenomenon is often seen in paranoids wrestling with a burning hatred of their presumed persecutors. Their very purpose for being is their pursuit of revenge and they will often, like Iago, bide their time awaiting the moment and opportunity to strike their blow. As we said above, the blow may be verbal or physical, depending on the nature of the individual, and, it may be leaked far in advance of planned intent if the hater senses some unexpected, unbearable provocation. The act itself, despite the degree of its violence, may only be representative of a larger and more pervasive imbalance in the sufferer. We don't doubt that the fanatical shooter at the military base is paranoid with a fixed delusional system which, typically, draws upon the societal issues of the day for its content. His world and his relationship to it is defined by his paranoia. There is no room for the innocent, blameless event; everything that happens has alter meaning. That's why it often is difficult to identify a logical inciting cause for the outbreak of violent behavior beyond the confines of a stable, compensated, ideational content, the delusional system itself. At best, the act can only be understood by others if the dynamics of the delusional system are known. We believe the shooter is delusional but probably no more so than is necessary to be a religious fanatic politically driven, as likely most Jihadists are. The "driven" part of it owes its energy to the obsession it commands in the sufferer's mind. In this case, an obsessional hatred. Such, we suspect, is the case with the shooter. But just why he decided to act as he did when he did remains unclear.

A certain parallel may be seen in President Obama's address to the nation on the tragedy. *His* leakage symptom was his two-minute indictment of White America in the abuse of Native Americans; i.e., the Indians. It was a symptom which, in the absence of a scripted delivery, slipped out, so to speak, and it calls attention to a likely larger network of his thinking which is obsessional on the point that America should be punished. We think that those around him know this about him, thus the fairly mandatory use of the tele-prompter to reduce the likelihood of such leaks, an oblique indicator of the intensity of his obsession. Hence likely also his reluctance to send more troops to Afghanistan for, after all, America is to be punished, beaten, and not allowed to be victorious in another world challenge. His sympathies flow, we suspect, in the same direction of those who also feel America should be punished and defeated. Indeed, he did later lament the death and wounding of those soldiers in Texas, but his words had a hollow, disingenuous, perhaps coldly elegiac ring, much like what many a victorious GI felt after the German surrender in 1945 upon seeing the massive and extensive destruction of Germany and its people: a terrible thing to have hap-pened, but without doubt necessary and right.

And we suspect there will be more leakage symptoms since obsessions of a paranoid type need to be fed and validated in order to sustain the sufferer's sense of self, particularly an exalted sense of self which would otherwise sour for lack of purpose. President

Obama will demand consensual validation to satisfy and extend his obsession and will likely get much of that validation legislated into law, law criminalizing what America has long stood for. More to come on that point, but for the time being let's note that the gun-man's supervisors and superiors who knew of his aberrant thinking and did nothing about it in obedience to certain civil sanctions are little different from President Obama's political colleagues who know of his driven predilections and do nothing about it out of obedience to partisan sanctions which, dutifully, they legislate into law for all and offer as protection of the people and love of country.

A strange love indeed.

16 November 2009

XV

The Vision of Chicken Little

It is perhaps superfluous to call attention to something so visibly before us, something that has become an ordinary ubiquity among so many others of our daily givens. Yet, expressly so, that very "something" might bear particular notice inasmuch as it, like a noise level we're accustomed to, is heard more clearly when a merciful silence intrudes. Thus, that "something" just might be better reckoned if openly positioned against the backdrop of what it specifically is not. Plus, if such comparison is at all necessary for giving correction to our usual perspective in accounting what we do and its meaning, there then is reason to consider why any deflection in our notational habitude occurs at all. But such deflections do occur and they are called different things in different settings. At the simplest it is called *neglect*, much as one sees in certain cerebral stroke victims whose affliction takes the form of their neglect of an entire side of their perceptual field, depending on which cerebral hemisphere is affected. They can indeed perceive the neglected portion of their surround, and actually do so—they are not blind to any portion of their visual field—but it is simply more a matter of failure to include that aspect of it in their automatic sensory and cognitive grasp of their world. It is as though they just choose not to heed that particular side of their surroundings. The word *automatic* is key here and it denotes the non-intentional character of the process. It is simply the result of damage to lateralizing brain circuits with a resulting deflection in attention set. And the victims are only dimly aware of it.

However, a similar net effect can come of action by the ego defense mechanism known as *denial*. Here, some specific aspect of one's reality is simply not allowed conscious recognition. The process is genuinely unconscious, but it is intentional. The specific element being denied along with the very process by which such is achieved remains on an unconscious level; that which is being denied is genuinely present as mental content but it is forcefully forbidden of conscious recognition. We say "forcefully" in view of the protest and fury that comes of identifying the process to its practitioner and forcing into awareness that which had been embargoed from conscious address. This mental process is also pathologic but it is fairly common in its lesser forms. *Denial* is considered the most primitive of the ego defense mechanisms.

Avoidance is another means whereby open assessment of one's practices and their meaning is prevented. The results and consequences of some given behavior are there to behold, but they are quite consciously ignored. Such a practice is more or less conscious, and it depends in part upon an intact capacity to discern precisely what it is that must not be noted. This practice is also common, perhaps even vital in lubricating the wheels of social intercourse. It is usually the device whereby former enemies are able to be enlisted in an alliance newly seen to be mutually profitable. At its best it is seen as forgiveness; at its worst it is seen as perfidy. It does not necessarily depend upon stealth because it can be jointly endorsed, and its utility can usually be justified through the use of another defense mechanism known as *rationalization*, one also seen as pathologic but much less so than out and out denial.

All of the above practices depend in large part on their effectiveness in deceiving, and deceiving foremost their very practitioners; fooling the self, so to speak. If they similarly deflect the thinking of others, so much the better. But self-deception is their prime purpose, and the less conscious the effect, the better. However, when the alter meaning and purpose of one's practices and behavior depend on a measure of consciously contrived stealth for deceiving *others* an important line is crossed. Such behavior is then no longer a matter of relatively innocent, everyday psychopathology, and it cannot be seen as a product of honest, ostensibly well-intentioned persuasion; it now becomes a matter of frank morality. In such practice, the deception of others, but specifically to exempt oneself, becomes primary.   True, one can believe that a given deception might sometimes serve a great good, such as in espionage, but the deception, to be effective, must be consciously contrived, disguised, and directed against others for it to be effective. The major device used in this practice is the *lie*.

Further, all of the above practices have in common a means of addressing a reality found otherwise unsuitable. Without their employment, that reality would require an open mode of address whose honesty would be even more unacceptable to the purposes of its practitioners though some form of address remains compulsory, forbidding a frank out and out rejection of the entire matter for fear of transforming a difficult situation into a wretched one. Thus, the storied and venerable double-bind colloquially known as being between a rock and a hard place. Life does not stint in providing us with reminders of such binds, but nor does Life often relax its demand that we satisfy our needs, many of which cannot be openly declared. But despite their seeming variety and differences all the above practices share not only a common theme, that of side-stepping some unacceptable aspect of reality, but have also a directional sense of what that reality is, plus often an appreciation of just how much distortion the reality will tolerate. Hence there is premium placed on the availability and readiness of a certain store of pleasing *plausibilities* available to apply in the resolution effected. We know this practice as *illusion,* as is often seen in ardent followers. But in an important particular its allowable resolutions collectively differ from an ultimate and much more extreme means of addressing an unacceptable reality, and that method is flight into *psychotic decompensation.* Here we mean that its sufferer, in address of a stressful reality, has, through a combination of psychologic, biologic, and sociologic vulnerabilities, broken with reality and proceeds to formulate a distinct, passionate, highly personalized, and usually fantastic conception of the nature and purpose of the stressful reality, but also along with it a piercing insight into what is ordained to be the stress' resolution. The device used here is the *delusion*.

Delusions, aside from policies, are usually highly personalized, and they often take their stamp from the character of the mental decompensation itself. In the process of mental decompensation the sufferer traverses several distinct stages before delusion formation is achieved. These stages usually include loss of appreciation of everyday rational causality, loss of the distinction between self and non-self, and loss of a balanced connection with the elements of the everyday world, elements both human as well as non-human. The sufferer typically feels the world is actually coming to an end, and he is correct in so far as *his* world of sane mental function is concerned. But because of loss of the self/non-self distinction he believes that it is the *world* which is coming to an end and that he's the only who appreciates the magnitude of the mounting calamity. It is generally at this point, the point of terrifying dissolution, that the sufferer achieves understanding of the true nature of the problem. The understanding usually comes in the form of an epiphany, or a profound enlightenment, and frequently in the form of divine visitation carrying a message of revelation and mission. The sufferer usually then achieves a great sense of relief as well as an elevating beatitude, typically seen as grandiosity, to flavor his singular understanding of the meaning and purpose of his transcendent experience. His mission is now ordained and it usually involves saving the world from what its doom would otherwise be since the rest of the human race seems so woefully unaware of what awaits it. Moreover, salvation can come only through the ministry of the now "chosen" one, himself. The sufferer has now achieved a stabilizing *delusion* which becomes the linchpin of his identity and life purpose.

Hence, the delusion is a form of restitution of the self by way of re-establishment of the sufferer's mental function keyed to a cosmic, often divine, destiny. It can have large persecutory elements, and often does, as additional justification of his mission, but the grandiosity is ever-present as the primary vehicle of ministry. And it is passionately defended for those very reasons. The grandiosity's sustaining energy usually comes of its own ministry in much the same way recovering alcoholics stand a much better chance of staying dry if they participate in programs given to the rescue of active problem drinkers. When they run out of active drinkers to rescue they themselves frequently return to drinking, their problem no longer conveniently externalized, and their redemption no longer in effect.

But a *delusion* can also be nourished by an accommodating society if it comes at a time of national stress and regression. In the delusion's message of hope and promised restitution it may even acquire, through the process of collective legal and social institutionalization, an aura of societal, even global, predestination and therewith recruit a following of fervid adherents who believe that salvation is truly at hand. Regrettably, it would nonetheless still bear the stamp of insanity, the usual handmaiden of moral and social breakdown. And, of course, it could also become politically very useful.

Now what does all this have to do with Chicken Little and her Vision? Just about everything. We may never know what peculiar stresses Chicken Little had been experiencing while pecking away at her lunch such that an acorn falling on her head opened her to the delusion that the sky was falling, but we do know that she never questioned the accuracy of her insight or the validity of her mission: nothing less than immediately rushing to tell the king would do. In her need to do so she enlists along the way the impassioned assistance of Ducky Lucky, Goosey Loosey, Turkey Lurkey, and assorted others, each contributing to the frenzy of the moment and its mounting hysteria. Something has to be done right away or else all are doomed. No one questions her conviction that the sky is falling, or her mission to keep it from doing so. She and her following are of one mind in their purpose.

But along the way in their mission to notify the king of the coming calamity they meet up with Foxy Woxy. Now, Foxy Woxy doesn't see the situation as do Chicken Little and her following; he sees it as one of great opportunity, not danger. He also recognizes that a pretended belief in the necessity of their mission would do wonders for fulfilling his own secret agenda which is to make a meal of Chicken Little and her following. He says all the correct things, and even offers helpful hints as he journeys along with them in the mission which has now covertly become more his than theirs, though they, in their hysteria, know only their own mission, an arrangement which is just fine with Foxy Woxy, who now needs to do little more than to wait for his reward to come of their hapless endeavor. The upshot of the story is that he manages to devour some of her following. With help, Chicken Little escapes, but, for it all, becomes none the wiser as to the folly of her mission and its cost.

The story is an ancient one, out of Africa, and has acquired many variations along the way. It has been woven into theatrical productions, video cartoons, even studio animations. The prevailing moral, however, remains about the same: the exploitation of simple and credulous others caught up in the hysteria of some fantastic belief and whipped into a frenzied rush to salvation.

Beyond psychiatric hospitals, where do we see this phenomenon commonly played out? The answer seems to lie in those settings in which the masses are most responsive to the vagaries of their leaders, self-appointed or otherwise. Moreover, when a self-ordained leader, particularly one of messianic stripe, is legitimized by popular choice, the setting is ripe for just such a phenomenon to occur, perhaps even to the point of inevitability. Typically, the populace is slow to realize where it is being taken, but the Foxy Woxies are keen to evolving opportunities along the way. And the leader, in the tradition of Chicken Little, is unmindful of the general cost to all. Adjusting locale along with the names of the main characters and one has a dead ringer for our esteemed and storied legislative system, especially on the Congressional level. Especially now. And most especially in view of the legislative urgencies afoot.

It has been said that while tyranny empowers the madman, democracy empowers the fool. This sentiment does an injustice to democracy in that democracy, as it is applied in America, demonstrably empowers both the madman *and* the fool in their implacable pursuit of each other. And all serve, even those who just stand and wait, such as Foxy Woxies are inclined to do, as the passion play works its magic. Let's say a Chicken Little divines, while in fevered apoplexy, that the world is coming to an end but that, providentially the one and only route to salvation has been shown. This particular Chicken Little thus has the moral duty and divine mandate to pass his enlightenment on to his flock. His reasoning demands that he make known to his flock those evident and visible indicators of impending Doom as might earlier have escaped their notice. So he points out the signs and explains their meaning. The flock initially becomes concerned because the signs—environmental, social, political, and even economic—seem indeed plausible. That word again. Hence there is a gathering sense of threat, much as Chicken Little proclaims. Soon, with each member's concern recruiting and amplifying that of the other, the concern rises to the level of popular unrest. Then, in no time at all a calamity is proclaimed. Soon enough an activist movement is formed, and its demands for emergency measures are now heard. New procedures and practices are to be enacted, and without delay. In the meantime the Foxy Woxies are intently watching, perhaps even helpfully guiding the gathering frenzy along. They soon enough gauge that a most favorable time to introduce certain procedures and practices of their own is at hand to be offered as part of the salvation effort but which practices and procedures would never be approved by the populace when in a sober and unburdened frame of mind. So, the Foxy Woxies, in sustaining the sense of crisis, are now so much better positioned to achieve their ends. They also remain unmindful and uncaring of the general cost to all, and slyly so.

Needless to say, our little story implies that Chicken Little can be any one of our leaders, past or present, nourishing a grand illusion, or worse, a delusional belief that he is ordained by inscrutable forces, usually Divine, to save the world, or its environment, or his country, or his people from the danger of eternal damnation. And the Foxy Woxies are our legislators given to dissemblance, obliquity, and, when necessary, out and out lying to secure their enactments which otherwise would never pass the general muster. But one thing our leaders and our legislators agree upon is that *crisis* is the medium in which their practices work best. Thus, crisis is to be awaited, cultivated, nourished, and, when necessary, purposely fabricated to have the process of governance, as we know it, proceed more effectively, as it were. Certainly, no crisis is ever to be wasted, it has been said. And, oddly, as Fate would have it, we note a varied sampling of just such initiatives before us even as we speak.

The man on the street might allow that such legislative hooliganism does occasionally occur, but yet still prefer to think that it is more the uncommon exception rather than the rule. However, such seems not to be the case at all. For example, the public has recently become aware, perhaps reluctantly, that literally thousands of riders—"earmarks"—can be attached to Congressional bills loudly proclaimed as emergent in nature. The riders, by virtue of their attachment to the emergent bill, are taken out of the normal, due process of legislative disquisition preparatory to an open vote by the taxpayer's representative. A vote for the emergent bill automatically becomes a vote for the rider. Perhaps even worse, such practice often underwrites transfer of municipal, county, and state responsibility to the federal government, again without say so by the collective citizenry, not to mention specifically the citizenry who dutifully pay the taxes. To oppose such chicanery would, in some cases, result in untoward opposition to agreed-upon, good-faith emergent legislation designed to address some national crisis, real or otherwise. For example, who in this day and age would oppose a National Defense appropriations bill, especially now when we actually have troops in the field combating terrorists intent on destroying this nation? No sensible, responsible citizen, for sure. But would that citizen support as well an attached rider authorizing the federal government to allocate several million public dollars for the construction of a Visitors' Center in one of our larger cities? A Visitors' Center on a National Defense bill? A Visitors' Center which is, if ever actually constructed, rightfully the fiscal responsibility of local authorities, such as municipal, or county, or even state? Would the taxpayers of, say, Cincinnati, or Atlanta, blithely agree to their national defense dollars being used to build a Visitors' Center in, say, San Francisco? Such a bill could never stand on its own, involving as it does a demand that taxpayers across the nation preferentially fund a very fiscally presumptuous city in its tourism enterprise. Here again the man on the street may see such legislative duplicity as an uncommon event not at all representative of the whole. But is it truly uncommon when a Congressional bill acquires literally *thousands* of such riders? There is just too much here to *deny*, and there is much to say that such is now the standard legislative practice in Congress and not at all the exception. The result is that the taxpayer, though providing an underwriting treasury, is effectively removed from the legislative process as entire sectors of his enfranchisement are given over to centralized authority. A creeping disenfranchisement, one might say. But worse yet, the average citizen, out of simple ignorance, or neglect, or avoidance, or denial, or, yes, even narrow self interest, seems not to mind at all, especially so if in any way he believes that crisis is upon him, because, after all, who can disagree that security and comfort are so much more satisfying than Liberty with its array of duties and responsibilities which, after all, can quite conveniently be ceded to centralized federal authority, an accommodation especially favored by those who expect the expense of their lifestyle to be underwritten by the national treasury, a pursuit particularly characteristic of that state with the city so eager to erect a new Visitors' Center.

It might be said that not all our legislators are given to such fiscal chicanery in the service of special interests. Perhaps. However, it is likely that most legislators would indeed write off such dissembling practices as "just politics," and the average taxpayer would likely accept that blandishment for having heard it so many, many times in the course of his growing up to full taxpayer status. Such buttering would be exactly akin to calling treasonous espionage directed against this nation as "just a bit of hide and seek," something the responsible citizen would not likely accept no matter who said it. But all politicians, especially the professional ones, are skilled at glossing over their dissembling practices, and they also know that oblique praise and admiration await those singularly skilled at it, as in the case of one of our recent Presidents. But *all* legislators? All! And either by commission or omission. True, not all legislators are as energetic in the pursuit in that practice as some others, but you will never, never, ever hear a legislator stand up in clear and loud denunciation of such practice, especially if such a stand would repudiate and indict members of his *own* party. He just might condemn such practices in others, but never in his own. To do so would be to break his own rice bowl, as the Chinese quaintly put it, for there would be no telling when he himself might need some special legislative accommodation for his own purposes. Such a legislator might perhaps plead to the lesser crime of his being negligently silent in his opposition to the practice, but this would be much the same as believing oneself less guilty of a robbery for having been merely the driver of the getaway car and not actually the one who pointed the gun. No. All! Plus, this collusion, which takes the shape of membership in an elitist order far removed from the life of the legislator's constituency, redefines integrity as obedience to an honored code whereby all members of that order are to be each other's enablers in the practice of such legislative obliquity. Disagreement among themselves is allowed on the various specifics of a bill, but not on the tailored ethics underwriting the manner of achieving the bill's passage. One might liken the scene to that of professional athletes, such as baseball

110

players, maybe professional wrestlers, who are members of teams or who comprise a league. The contenders play each other in hotly contested games to entertain the fans but actually are colleagues in their going comradeship, in their devotion to the game, and in their loyalty to the ethic of the sport. The fans provide the revenue to support the overall arrangement expressly for their own entertainment and in hope of their team's victory. The players hope for victory as well, but they also can find it within themselves to gather together, winners and losers cheek by jowl, after the game for a beer and back-slapping camaraderie in their supervening loyalty to each other. That's why an impeached President was never tried for his crimes. But here again, the average citizen seems not to mind at all as long as his righteous indignation and moral outrage are not provoked by his being taxed for the open benefit of grossly undeserving others. It seems fair play is to be observed even in vagrancy and misfeasance; that is, if it is freely collaborative and profitable. But, regrettably, this perspective serves as imprimatur for corruption on all levels, and soon there is the sense that everybody, the governed as well as the governing, are serving a tedious but obligatory charade, and thus nourishing a pernicious legislative and civil ambience which happens to be one of the first signs of societal degeneracy (See Entry XI). But, with that note in mind it just might be said that our legislators are perhaps doing exactly what we citizen taxpayers covertly intend of them, just as long as we don't have to know about it.

Here the term "elite" comes into focus. Of late the term has taken on a pejorative reference. Has the term itself undergone some degradation? The Founding Fathers, learned and graceful men that they were, were truly elite in the intended and affirmative meaning of the word. They led for the benefit of the people and were willing to accept any penalty to come of it. And many paid heavily. They were truly unique. They measured well above the common man in their reach as well as in their grasp, and their virtue stood tallest of the time. And the common man knew it, honored it, and modeled himself by it as best he could. But those Founders were as few as

111

their uniqueness was rare, as one could expect. Plus, it was all a very long time ago when equality was seen, and accepted, as applying only to equality under the law. Now, our "elite" ordain that equality is to be seen as applying well beyond founding law, even at the expense of a founding Constitutional precept. The result is that the societal challenge of these times seems to be the eradication of as many embarrassing individual differences and their derivative inequalities as might resist and dilute the absolute egalitarianism rooting of certain political agendas awaiting their moment. Given that our current legislators, in their elitism, are not quite unique and that their virtue is not at all towering, it does seem that they, in their need to reassure their constituencies, do piously feature a pro forma political rectitude but one which distinctively abhors open and searching analysis of actual policy or purpose, public or personal, for fear of the execrable sound it would make in the open air. Whatever else it may or may not be, seeing our legislators, our leaders, and sundry important others as "elite" and the rest of us as no more or less graceful and virtuous than each other, or even caring to be, is unquestionably Simon-pure, wall to wall, affirmative egalitarianism. In effect, our "elite," in their pursuit of a politically correct egalitarianism, endeavor to enlist us into an institutionalized, communal mediocrity intolerant of individual enterprise and its rewards as both fiscally reprehensible and societally immoral. But, how could we then ever become better than we are? And to where ought we be led? Washington feared that were we so inclined, then our becoming "a grazing multitude" surely awaited; that is, until the sky really fell.

06 January 2010

112

XVI

Hidden Roots

It has come to everyone's attention that President Obama distinctly avoids calling the terrorists *Islamic* terrorists. Nor does he call them *Muslim* terrorists. He clearly prefers to call them *Al Qaeda* terrorists. Yet they are all Muslims, converts or natural born, and fanatically religious ones at that. They apparently feel that they are on a mission in the name of Islam, a mission aimed at destroying America as an evil, infidel nation assaulting the followers and the teachings of Allah. These terrorists are at least equally intent on destroying Israel, and for much the same reason though the Koran quite specifically names the Jews as infidels dutifully to be killed. Hence the motives at play here are essentially religious in nature though political ideology is also at hand but lesser in its thrust as is typical in nations ruled by clerics. This is much the case in the Muslim world.

To limit reference to the Al Qaeda terrorists as merely members of a criminal activist organization when they are fundamentally a militant arm of Islamic theology approaches a study in denial at its very best, or worst (See Entry XV). No one really believes that Al Qaeda is just an independent group of activists playing out nationalistic fervor to register grievances against either invasive American capitalism or local American military operations, or both. True, such American initiatives may be cited as provocative of the *Jihadists'* belligerence but, despite the separate and distinct, non-theologic purposes of the initiatives themselves, they are regarded as attacks upon all Islam. As said above, nations ruled by clergy certainly do not set commercial or military issues apart from religious imperatives since the sense of nation in such a setting is at one with its religious identity. Thus any infidel military operation against any Islamic group for any reason is an attack against *all* Islamic peoples. Similarly with arching Western capitalist ventures buffeting Islamic society. For example, during the days of the Holy Roman Empire an alien attack against Germany, let's say, would be seen as an attack against the Holy Roman Empire, and if the attackers were anything but Catholic the attack would be seen as against all Catholicism even if the attackers insisted that their goal was not only local but also strictly political in purpose with religious differences to be honored. But the sense of separate "nationhood" in the days of the Holy Roman Empire had little meaning and designated no more than a regional distinction carrying no sovereignty as such whatever. The Empire was not at all a union of independent, sovereign states, but a loose collection of respondent provinces and principalities over which the church in Rome ruled. Assigning issues a "national" reference had little meaning to the Holy See because religion and its imperatives ruled over all. Thus, non-Catholics contesting some issue with Germany was seen by Rome as simply an assault upon some region of the Holy Roman Empire and its faithful.

But the West eventually moved away from that collectivist thinking with the beginning of the Renaissance when a founding nationalism began to take hold in the formation of nations as we know them today. Thus, in the Western world today an Algerian military operation against Spain would not likely be seen as an attack against Catholicism inasmuch as many of the attackers would likely themselves be Catholic, or even of Spanish descent. As parallel, one may recall Great Britain's dispute with Argentina over the Falkland Islands. Religion was not a part of the scene. Nation and national interests were.

This is not the case with Islam. It seems that any non-Islamic operation directed against a Muslim group is regarded as an attack on Islam itself. Whatever may be the moment's subtler background political and economic shadings, the collective religious position is inevitably held to be primary. Thus, to see it as otherwise is to appeal to irrelevance. To explain to the lowly activist, or the common

114

Islamic citizen, that our military operations against Al Qaeda are directed solely against terrorism, not Islam, would be about the same as fourteenth century invading Turks explaining to the Christians of southeastern Europe that their motive was political and for material conquest only, and not directed against Christendom. Those four-teenth century Christians, especially the Holy See, would likely dis-miss such an attempt at exculpating distinction as itself a crime against the Trinity and proclaim the Turkish invasion of Europe to be a holy war against Christianity. And thus it so happened.

Al Qaeda, in the minds of Muslims, *is* Islam in much the same sense that the Crusaders of the eleventh century *were* Christianity, each the more militant arm of their respective theologies. But even if such a distinction between a people and their more activist, militant group is a genuinely definable one, action against that activist group is likely not to be seen by their people as action *not* directed at them as well. Even though effort was made to have the Germans know that the Allies were at war with the Nazi regime and not necessarily with the German people themselves, few Germans took solace and comfort from that reassurance as Germany and its people were bombed and blasted into submission by the Allies in their defeat of the Nazis. At that time the Nazis *were* Germany of a particular stamp, hailed by the German people with resolute and tragic loyalty. After the war was over there were, of course, very few Germans to be found who had actually been genuine Nazis. They were now simple, traditional Germans once again.

History is rich in examples of canted refusal to recognize the whole despite how telling the part may be (See Entry VIII). Certainly there are diplomatic and economic reasons why refusal to do so is often seen to be necessary. Nevertheless, such efforts just about always come off as pathetically Chamberlain in nature, and risible as well. True, it is indeed within the teachings of diplomacy and bargaining that adopting the rôle of the fool has its usefulness, but it never has lasting benefit, simply buying time as it does, and it always encourages the adversary who unfailingly sees it as a victory over a beguiled or cowering enemy.

With all this history upon us, why does President Obama maintain a position which requires that Al Qaeda not to be seen as Islamic enemy combatants, much less the militant arm of Islam, but rather as an independent group of criminal activists bent on opposing America here at home as well as abroad? And why does he not openly detail his reasons for thinking so? Simply designating them as independent activists, as he has done, just does not do justice to the reality or the scope of the issue. Plus, such a simplistic address as is now his official stand is likely seen by Al Qaeda as at least avoidant and perhaps even as national retreat. Maybe even sympathy.

As is usual with such a questionable posture the proposed reasons are likely multiple and each carries a measure of verisimilitude. Perhaps as a result they do add up to a certain sufficiency though separately they lack conclusiveness for want of necessity. For example, in the interest of sustaining a useful amity it would appropriately be politic to avoid identifying generic Islam as the sustaining force of Al Qaeda, for such a stance would oblige us to regard official Islam, wherever, as a co-belligerent in Al Qaeda's operations. Yet, that's exactly what everybody sees the real matter to be anyway. But is official avoidance of open recognition of such necessary? Could ever such avoidance, or denial, of that reality be sufficient? Hardly. It certainly would be nothing new to have the major belligerents— America and Islam—openly recognized as such but with the rules of engagement displacing actual military combat to politically more convenient precincts. It was no secret back in 1950 that Soviet Russia and its ally, Red China, were at odds with America in its rôle as leader of the Western World. North Korea, as the instrument of the Soviet block, invaded South Korea not only to annex that country into the Communist system but also to eradicate American presence on the Asian mainland. America, and the UN, resisted, and we had the Korean War. American forces did not engage Soviet forces, at least not officially, nor did they invade China. The confrontation was

116

contained in Korea and limited to American and U.N. opposition to the Asian representatives of the Communist coalition. One might have worked at seeing North Korea and China as rogue nations bearing only nominal identity with Russian interests, but everybody knew better: North Korea and China were the Communist forces of the moment and spoke for the entire Marxist system. The parallel with Al Qaeda is there to see.

One could also say that President Obama is necessarily keen to the economic forces which shape the political and military scene, oil clearly serving as the key feature. That notion has its own well-established plausibility which both participants honor and do so for essentially the same reason: the Middle East needs the American oil market, and America needs Middle Eastern oil. But does America really need that particular oil? With the current American political parties and their controlling constituencies structured as they are, apparently yes. It is well known that America could, on its own, satisfy its oil energy needs for many decades to come, but to do so would offend constituencies which hold that additional drilling locally would pose *more* of a threat to America than does militant, extremist Islam. There is solace in this position for those who are inclined to rationalize in protection of the environmentalist agenda, derivative as it is of Edenic illusions, that the world would indeed come to an end if man-made pollution were not prevented (See Entry XV). Certainly, President Obama could easily draw upon this mind-set in crediting his reasons for not indicting extremists elements of Islam as the motive force behind Al Qaeda because to do so would employ too broad a brush for the canvas he wants to keep small, though the rank and file of Al Qaeda are visibly quite representative of the larger Islamic world and its several nations.

So why is President Obama seemingly so fixed on keeping Al Qaeda terrorism separate from Islam, at least in his official thinking? The reason could of course be based on pursuit of a balanced policy for protecting diplomatic channels in avoidance of having the conflict flare up into climactic proportions—America against Islam—and in

117

preventing such sustain a useful détente with larger Islam while at the same time having limited American forces abroad engage in military combat with only Al Qaeda, though carefully never quite decisively for fear of provoking larger Islam into open, escalating conflict. To designate Muslim ideology and policy as the driving and sustaining forces behind Al Qaeda terrorism would oblige him as Commander-in-Chief of our nation to address Al Qaeda's threat, not just on the field of *its* choosing, enjoying so the benefit of having the initiative, but at its very *source*. This would require a measure of initiative nowhere in evidence at this time in his administration since it is fairly clear that President Obama is simply not the kind of Commander-in-Chief to lead such an effort, something the Jihadists know all too well.

However, with all that being said of the need to juggle contending urgencies while espousing a policy of protecting America and its interest, plus sustaining channels of communication with dissidents, and certainly to satisfy electoral forces, the question still remains as to why President Obama refuses even remotely to associate Al Qaeda terrorism with Islam when the terrorists are almost exclusively, if not all, Muslims? The actual answer seems not to derive from the international and domestic contingencies which come into play, but from within President Obama himself.

We all know that President Obama had two fathers, a biologic father he allegedly saw only once, after infancy, and a stepfather by whom he was reared at least till age ten, during which years he acquired a Muslim half-sister. His biologic father was reared Muslim and remained so till a young man, and the stepfather, an Indonesian, was a practicing Muslim his entire life. President Obama spent the predominance of his childhood years in Muslim Indonesia and was registered as a Muslim in the schools he attended. His mother received a Ph.D. in Indonesian studies, essentially Muslim studies.

It has long been held by the academic arm of the Catholic Church, and it was specifically stated by one of its great early educators, Aquinas, that if the child is taught by them for the first twelve

118

years of his life "he is ours forever." There appears to be a certain validity in this premise. We might note that for ten of those twelve formative years President Obama was reared Muslim, either by design or association; to wit, a Muslim Community, a Muslim step-father, a distant and idealized biologic father who was born Muslim but later supposedly an atheist though he names his son Barack *Hussein* Obama in keeping with Muslim tradition, a political activist paternal grandfather, plus a radical and restless mother committed to Muslim Indonesian studies. And add to all this his everyday Muslim playmates. The influence had to be telling. Moreover, President Obama, in those formative years, likely seen as a different, biracial little boy in an alien community and in search of where and to whom he belonged, must have clutched tenaciously to the image of his father, a Muslim for much of his life and the man he saw only once, for in Obama's memoirs, entitled *Dreams of My Father,* his father figures so much more prominently than does his mother. The identification process was likely directed at that image, the only one in President Obama's immediate family that physically looked like him.

The upshot, we suspect, is that President Obama, in his heart of hearts, is Muslim in his dearest attachments, and that for him to identify Jihad terrorism with Islam would not only indict Islam but would also provoke conflict as much in the larger political sphere as among crucial elements of his own personal identity, an apostasy which could not be permitted, especially so since his current portrayal of self, while it likely reflects aspects of his unsettled childhood, may be more representative of a trait transmitted by his mother who seemingly followed a restless search for a more durable, stable, and integrated sense of self than she perhaps had ever achieved. Indeed, President Obama's seemingly kindred pursuit in this regard may bear on the reason question recurrently arises as to who he really is, where was he actually born, and so forth. Perhaps it also helps to understand why his stand on Muslim terrorism is so very similar to that of the American Muslim Community: they never as a group and rarely as individuals openly oppose Jihadist terrorism, but rather remain quietly neutral. Or worse, covertly endorse it.

18 January 2010

XVII

Sarah Budd

Over the past several years Sarah Palin, former governor of Alaska and Republican Vice-Presidential candidate in 2008, has become something of an American *cause célèbre*. Her civic accomplishments are signal, to be sure, but her notoriety is fanned more by the standard media's ongoing antipathy towards her, and even toward her family. One simply has to wonder why the media continues to focus its enmity on her even though she is no longer on the political stump as a current, standing candidate for any particular office. She is indeed a contributor to the present American political scene, but so are many others, especially incumbent office-holders who are so much more deserving of critical scrutiny though apparently regarded as of lesser importance. And perhaps also a lesser danger.

Moreover, when she was an office-seeker she drew more media criticism than did her running-mate Presidential candidate who set the platform she embraced in the campaign. Indeed she had personally demonstrated her commitment to one of the planks of that platform in setting the composition of her very own family. So her advocacy had to be accounted as more than mere rhetoric aimed at what was to be expected of others. Hence, her credibility was unequaled in the political arena of the day. One would thus have expected a certain credit to come her way, perhaps even from those of the opposition who officially held character to be a desideratum in any one seeking such high office, differences in policy and political perspective granted. But such was not the case, not with the opposing candidates and certainly not with the standard media. The opposing candidates, now elected office-holders, have generally moved on to other preoccupations, but not the media, which continues its campaign against her, and, as said, even against her family. The issue has to draw upon more personal elements than mere political differences given that there are many others at hand who share her opinions but who are spared the media's wrath. How can this be when the scene is complicated by her being adored by so many others who seem unshaken by the media's attacks on her and perhaps whose devotion to her is encouraged thereby? The media's ongoing assault upon her is unquestionably something less than journalistic; rather, perhaps oddly, even symptomatic of some societal malady, maybe one classical enough to have claim in our literary heritage. Our better literary heritage.

For example, a case in point could be Herman Melville's novel, *Billy Budd*. The story is that of a young sailor, a foretopman; that is, a sailor whose duty station is at the top-most platform of the foremast of a ship. He is orphaned and illegitimate, and while at sea he is pressed into service on a British man-of-war from his merchant ship, *Rights of Man*, where he is adored by its crew for his innocence, his openness, and his remarkable and inexplicable charisma. Soon he is equally adored by the crew of the man-of-war as well. But the ship's Master-at-Arms, Claggart, develops an antagonism toward Billy and in time accuses him of inciting mutiny. Standing so falsely accused before the captain's inquiry, Billy strikes back at Claggart, accidentally killing him. The Captain, who understands that Billy is innocent of the charge of mutiny, holds that though Billy has killed a most evil Claggart, the law must be obeyed. The captain is torn, but sees that Billy, in his total goodness, is, in his own way, as dangerous as is evil. He exclaims that though Claggart was struck dead by an angel of God, yet the angel must hang.

As one can imagine, many interpretations of the story have been offered, certainly to include Biblical ones, but the overriding theme of good versus evil subtends all of them. Even more, the presence of goodness, coupled with an unwavering, complete belief in it and having the courage to live that belief stands as oblique criticism of those who have neither belief in goodness, nor the courage to account it in others, and are thus singularly vulnerable to evil. In effect, even the kindliest existence of goodness points an accusing finger at evil and its variations, though not at all purposely. But those who feel accused so are not to be calmed by any kindness intended but rather are more likely to be solaced only by their own vengefulness. Like Claggart, so to speak.

And so it seems with Sarah Palin and the media. She presents as one who is honest, open, and sincere. There is a simple kindness and goodwill about her and she apparently feels no need to shade it from view in favor of a canny and strategic circumspection. In effect, she seems to believe in herself and also in her open, direct approach to the world. There seems to be little uncertainty in her pursuit of goodness in herself and in others, no shortage of conviction that she can recognize it when it is at hand, and certainly no lack of courage for embracing it. She shows no trace of devious or selfish design and appears to be compassionate of others in general, even those not so kindly disposed in return. She seems to assess herself by the same standards she holds for others. And her charisma is unchallenged. And the topping given to this personal confection is that she is captivatingly pretty. In effect, she seems to give lie to the hoary, conventional wisdom that fitness for rule requires the ability to hate. Worse, now we may even no longer be able to see politics as Show Biz for the ugly.

All of this flies in the face of our common conception of the politician as one who is wily, skillfully dissembling, convincingly deceptive, and practiced at civil jugglery. But we do appreciate the appearance, and pretense, of honesty in our politicians and we seem ready to accommodate just about any chicanery and imposture designed to protect that appearance and pretense. We truly know better, and we know that our politicians are exquisitely vulnerable to evil, as our history has repeatedly shown, but the illusion of honesty and rectitude is important to protect. But this is exactly what is at risk when Sarah Palin is around. Her mere presence points a finger at what her political colleagues, loyal or otherwise, are truly not, and the reactive vengefulness of the opposition and its supporting media reminds us that Claggart is not really dead and that Sarah Palin is not immune to being falsely accused. Plus, there certainly are those who would say that her mystique is actually more a matter of her being quaint rather than compelling. Perhaps, as regards her openness and simple grace, but there remains the undeniable phenomenon that not only does she endure, but that she also seems to gather more and more following even though not actively on the stump. Her appeal continues to grow, even in the quagmire of cynicism we know as our political environment. Perhaps it is because people see in her not only what they have long lost sight of in their leaders *but what they would like to preserve in themselves*, a sentiment some might see as approaching a kind of civil mutiny but one which just might allow the people to feel that they themselves would then be less vulnerable to evil and its Claggarts. Who knows, the people, in departure from the media and its favorites, might come to believe that character is not at all unrelated to policy, a notion too readily discounted by most of the media and almost all politicians.

26 January 2010

XVIII

The Prez's New Clothes

Once upon a time there was a wondrous land named Usa. It was the richest and most bountiful land in the world. It was also the land where people were free as nowhere else, and all its citizens knew opportunity as never before known in any other place in the wide, wide world. And its people were generous; they gave freely to other less fortunate people in distant lands and even welcomed those people to Usa's shores. And its people were kindly and eager to have others know opportunity as they, the Usans did, and also to become as industrious as they.

And Usa was ruled by the consent of its citizens, and its leaders were chosen by the people themselves, guided as they were by a founding charter of great wisdom and known as The Resolution by which the government conducted the affairs of the people. The one chosen by the people to protect this magnificent charter was known as The Prez, and over the years various persons were elevated to this exalted office for designated periods of time. The Prez was assisted in his duties by a Cabinet of Adherents endorsed by the citizens as the most skilled in their chosen fields.

And everybody of this wonderful land lived prosperously and were the envy of the people of all other lands.

But it came to pass that the people of Usa elected a Prez who promised them improvement in their already bountiful lot. This promise especially appealed to those Usans who had become so accustomed to their good fortune that they had begun to envy those Usans who had achieved so much more from the opportunities available to all. Soon the envious Usans began to yearn ever louder for more and more of what they had failed to acquire on their own.

The new Prez also promised Change. In like measure a multitude of the Usans were enamored of his vow to make the workings of their government clearer and more visible to everyone's notice. Many of the Usans, especially those grown envious, believed that such could only be helpful in improving upon their collective lot. So they had Hope.

But there were those of the new Prez's circle who knew that the changes intended were not what the people expected them to be, and they also knew that it was important the changes be brought about swiftly before the people had time to understand what those changes really were. It became very important to reassure the Usans that the changes to be enacted were truly in keeping with the provisions of The Resolution and also fully in keeping with the changes they had been prompted to expect and for which they had voted. But many Usans did wonder why they were not allowed to read the changes The Prez proposed and intended to accomplish.

Now The Prez was a man very much pleased with his elected purpose, but he also deeply believed that he was most especially chosen and thus ordained to achieve his vision not only of what all the Usans should have in equal measure but also what he believed the land should now be. He not only saw himself capable of taking the Usans beyond the mandates of The Resolution but also of emancipating himself from being merely the protector of it so that he might rule as its Redressor. Thus, his vision of the future was not truly the same as that of all the Usans but it was important for them to see him as The One arrived to take them where they wanted to go. Hence, how he appeared to them was a matter of great importance, for the more he looked like what they thought him to be the easier it would be for him to accomplish the changes he intended.

To achieve this he chose his Adherents carefully to include those who shared not only his goals but also his conviction that he was The One most providentially chosen for the redemption only he could deliver to the people of the land. His Adherents obeyed him devotedly but he knew that it would be conclusively grand and vital to his mission that the Usans, one and all, also obey him fully. A mere majority would not be satisfactory. To bring forth so splendid a communion of destinies he called upon his three most zealous and trusted Heralds—Cbsa, Nbca, and Abca—in hope of their taking to the Usans the message he needed them to hear in joyous witness of his ordained mission, and thus the land's coming redemption.

But these Heralds, unlike The Prez's Cabinet, were fully aware that he was not at all what he thought himself to be, though they did hold to his mission of converting the land anew, an ambition they had avouched long before The Prez's assumption. They knew it would be to their great benefit to nourish The Prez's preferred image of himself. So, to convince the Usans of his grandeur they vested him with the finest virtues and graces as could be imagined. They were so inspired in their coverage of him that soon more and more people of the land were convinced not only that the Prez was every bit what he and his Heralds said he was but also that any enactments come of his wisdom and vision would certainly be heaven-sent in view of the promised good to come of them. The Heralds were so ambitious in their mission that those Usans who were unconvinced, or who even had the slightest doubt of what they were told, were held to be of insufficient understanding, or worse, of foxy evil design. The Heralds knew well what was not to be seen, and thus became skilled beyond compare in weaving a cloak of splendor The Prez embraced as the self he professed, and thus the self he wanted all to see, believe, and love. And it did come to pass that The Prez was loved like no other of his kind.

But it so happened that in the province of Massa there was a Scot who had unshakeable faith in his own doubts. He doubted that The Prez was all what he believed himself to be or what so many Usans came to believe he was. This Scot of Massa also doubted the wisdom, judgment, and purpose of the new decrees The Prez would bestow upon the people. The Prez soon came to hear of Scot of Massa. The people of Massa also soon came to hear of him, and in time some citizens came to consider that though the Heralds had proclaimed it so that there could not possibly be any questioning of The Prez's mission, or that anyone could truly lack faith in his total goodness, or, worse, that any doubt as to his purpose could possibly exist, Scot of Massa spoke otherwise since in his very doubting he confirmed that not only he but also that all of his doubts did indeed exist. To wit, he thought and therefore he certainly was. In time, other persons in Massa began to wonder if they too should think, and be. Thus the Heralds saw need to redouble their efforts not only to have the people know and love The Prez as he needed, but also to have them embrace his vision with a lifting of their voices high in the paean of redemption known to all as the Honolulu Chorus. For a most happy ending to come of The Prez's blissful calling, the Heralds would together serve as joyous End Men.

And it soon came to pass that there was a grand contest between those citizens of Massa who favored *thinking* and those citizens who favored *feeling*. Those who favored thinking—they called themselves *Elephs*—saw their future and well-being so much the more promising the more they themselves managed it, while those who favored feeling—they called themselves *Donks*—held that their lot would be better served and assured were they to keep faith with what The Prez and his Heralds told them. The contest soon arrived at a telling and decisive tally which was watched carefully by The Prez, his Adherents, and especially by his three Heralds who had labored so hard to have everybody perceive The Prez according to what all were told to feel and see, inasmuch as *thinking* more precisely on the matter would likely leave The Prez laughably naked of endearing qualities.

The tally was counted with great care and no matter the many different ways it was reckoned the Elephs carried the day: doubting and thinking were now to be the standards used in viewing The Prez's figuration, and, much to his dismay, searching and open disclosure, even transparency, would indeed be the means whereby this would be accomplished. And the tally proclaimed Scot of Massa the new Censor, to censure as he deemed.

Word of the new view quickly spread throughout the land. The Heralds—Cbsa, Nbca, and Abca—had been exposed as to their design, just as was The Prez who now felt bereft of his glowing aura. The Prez then wax wroth with a furious anger which many citizens were loathe to countenance. And so the ranks of the Elephs grew.

The Heralds were quick to console The Prez and they soon set about tailoring for him a new visage as might enchant anew those to whom feeling still held more appeal than did thinking.

But the damage was done. Scot of Massa had exposed The Prez to open visibility by all and the Usans now realized that they had been led to see only what The Prez chose to believe of himself and only what he needed all others to believe him to be. And his Heralds had provided. But Scot of Massa had made The Prez and his guile too transparent and thus never ever again to know the blind faith of the people. The falsity of the Prez's preferred and public self had now been made clear not only to the Usans but very much to himself as well, an attribute not commonly present in those of his kind. But, truly, to that extent the Prez had indeed kept his vow of transparency and thus change of a very different, more revealing kind, was now before all.

08 February 2010

XIX

Paying the Piper

By now most people are aware that President Obama intends to redefine the purpose and place of government in the American scene and in so doing also redefine the very nation itself. In that regard he and his Cabinet resist using the term "Socialism" in spelling out the specifics of that re-definition, but their enactments leave no doubt that the prospectus and the goal of those re-definitions call for more governmental participation in all sectors of American society. Already, the Banking System, the Auto Industry, the Real Estate Market, the Insurance Business, and, lately, Education along with Health Care have felt the heavy tread of his dialectic. Elements of those sectors, through a combination of mismanagement and misadventure aided and abetted by federal incentive, invited the popular consensus that change was in order though that consensus, much of it come of the joint effects of electoral simplicity and pro-grammed disinformation, generally anticipated only a change based on improvement in the prevailing structure of American society. It seems that little thought was given to the possibility that a mandate for change, change presumed to be directed at achieving a more wholesome fulfillment of the national credo, could be exploited legislatively to force ideologic changes which would adversitively cut across the fabric of traditional American endeavor and especially the nation's exceptionalism.

And so here we are.

National indebtedness, now in extremis and purposely so, binds the citizen for generations to come to the task of sustaining a government chronically threatened by bankruptcy. The cost of main-taining a government so threatened, and its vast network of newly established social programs which, by design, keep it so, demands a redirection of individual endeavor at the open expense of personal enterprise which now, in the face of pre-emptive government claim, is to be seen as selfish, greedy, and unfair. Hence, the re-definition would include a re-thinking of the honored principles of free enterprise, personal liberty, private ownership, and certainly national purpose. This re-definition thus far faithfully traces the standard tenets of Socialist theory as it parallels the more comprehensive reach of conventional Communism.

Thus we are speaking of a major change in political ideology, a degree of change not anticipated and perhaps even less understood by a credulous electorate more likely motivated by grievance than by principle.

The key word here is "grievance." Dissatisfaction with some aspect of one's circumstances, fired by personal ambition, is basic to the concept of self-interest, and resolution of that dissatisfaction is its aim, whether individually or collectively pursued. It is not so much the number of persons active in this pursuit—all individuals are fundamentally so designed—or of any collaborative effort of any pursuit made in this regard; rather it will always be that any felt satisfaction, of whatever, prevail so as an innately individual and personal thing. We cannot escape the wellsprings of our deeper stirrings; at least not for long if life is to have any intrinsic, individual purpose, as it must. True, many people may, and do, join together in exercise of this pursuit, but the aim—satisfaction—remains a personal and exquisitely individual thing. It is thus that such persons' collaboration is simply the *means*, however well populated, but that individual satisfaction is innately and ultimately the *goal*. The group's collective sense of fulfillment can go only so far as its constituency's individual satisfaction is concerned because the character of that satisfaction depends ultimately on the individual and his relationship to his needs. In a word, while many may join together in some collective pursuit, let's say Justice for all, each person in that collaboration will have his own, individual need for doing so. Our need of Justice for all, which is likely generically similar to your need, will still and all ultimately be for our own personal reasons. The cry of Justice for all then becomes more a gathering point for a joined effort come of varied but kindred origins. It is wisely said that the individual can never be discounted; that is, if societal peril is to be avoided.

And so it is with ideologies as well. Many followers may identify with a specific ideology, along with its aim and practices for the accomplishment of some ostensible collective social, political, and economic good, but yet each adherent may have his own slant on why such and such a goal is good and personally deemed so.

President Obama has chosen Socialism/Communism as his ideologic format for accomplishing a particular and, for him himself, personally important change in American society as well as in the national identity. That much is clear. But why *that* particular political ideology? Why not Laissez-faire Democracy? Or Libertarianism? And, also, what do those two political ideologies have in common? A cursory glance at Webster will reveal that each ideology espouses the freedom of the individual—freedom from aggressive governmental control in daily affairs, freedom of individual enterprise, freedom to enjoy as desired the fruits of one's labor, freedom to choose and pursue the path of greatest personal promise, freedom to define one's own future as common chance will permit. In effect, an enshrinement of the individual's freedom to know life, liberty, and the pursuit of happiness as natural law might allow.

But, as we all know, Socialism/Communism does not permit such freedom. The individual and his self-interest—personal goals and the pursuit of their promised bounty—are subordinated to the group whose goals are defined by a controlling authority given to mass reckoning. Group goals define the individual's place and purpose in society, and individualism is to be seen as reactionary, deviant, and even immoral. Yet, every individual participant in President Obama's Socialist/Communist agenda is yet committed to his own personal agenda because of distinct, private reasons which are never spelled out openly in avoidance of the sour note such openness might

133

carry and quite possibly even lead to group fragmentation and personal alienation. So, premium is placed on endorsement of the more abstract and very general tenets of the official ideology with the result that public programming of its agenda always carries a nagging sense that the whole truth is not being told and that specific omissions are quite germane to the credibility of the ideology itself. Thus, specification of the root purpose of such and such an agenda is blandished along. And that's exactly what the Constitution forbids. Plus, it is generally conceded that Conservatives are usually known for their frankness of purpose and are often scorned by some for being too unequivocal for the delicate niceties of compassionate society, while the more lofty accents of the Liberal are just as often regarded as graceful obliquity more supportive of congenially collaborative congress. Perhaps that is why President Obama tends to speak in large, noble generalities and never allows himself to be specific on any issue—except by misadventure.

The question thus arises as to why President Obama embraces the Socialist/Communist doctrine at all and does so specifically to place other ideologies far beyond consideration? Plus, what is he actually trying to change and what is such change designed to correct in his own psychical economy and, ostensibly, also in that of our society? And why must the change involve all of American society? The answers must indeed be seminal.

One very available answer comes of the fact that President Obama is Black, the ramifications of which are detailed elsewhere (see Entry II). The ready and easy considerations here dwell on the nation's history of enslavement of the Black Man, plus the on-going alienation of the Black Man from the mainstream of American society along with the continued cultural, political, and economic impoverishment of the Black man in a ruling and flourishing White Western Society. There follows the need, personal as well as collective, to correct past wrongs this nation committed against the Black Man. In addition, there is the expectable commensurate need, again personal as well as collective, to seek national atonement for such in

134

the form of compensation as would help the Black Man achieve respect and credibility as a contributing citizen and thereby lift him to the status of equality in the reckoning of the American character. Such pursuits are nothing if not commendable and noble, and they are not new to the Black American scene. Indeed, national effort has not been stinting in social programs to achieve just such corrections, and extensive efforts at affirmation of the Black Man's needs have been institutionalized over the past several decades, extending over gen-erations, for correcting those imbalances penalizing him for so long. So why not continue in that vein, enrich those programs, define new areas of application, and enlarge outreach programs to recruit more Blacks in the enculturation process? In a word, give the Black Man as generous and as concerted a lift as would place him on par with his White and Oriental contemporaries. Commendable to say the least. So why is such an approach not pursued within the ideologic context of the America which has already established and implemented it thus far?

Because after fifty years of progressive and escalating legi-slative effort, and the expenditure of literally trillions of dollars in implementation of policy ranging from broad-based affirmative action across social, academic and industrial lines, to various per-sonal and family help programs—even to include food and nutrition subsidy on both the family as well as primary school level—the Black Man has essentially not improved his status or his relationship to mainstream America. The programs have been generous, even indulgent, but the Black Man's exploitation of them in the service of achieving social, educational and industrial parity with the White and Oriental sectors of American society has been wanting. Moreover, such a vast array of government subsidy and preference has never before in the history of this nation been awarded to any other racial or ethnic minority and for the simple reason that it was never asked for or even needed by those minorities for them to exploit the oppor-tunity American society offers to all. The Oriental, certainly, and to some extent, the recent Mexican minorities are a case in point. The more gifted and more enterprising members of the Black race have indeed moved forth as hoped, but, in general, the Black Man, as a race, has not moved far beyond custodial status requiring specifically designed government assistance in managing his needs in a modern scientific, industrial, technologic society. The reasons seen are detailed in earlier offerings (see Entry X).

How does this relate to President Obama's drive for substantive and ideologic change in our government's rôle and its relationship to its citizenry? It could indeed be said that President Obama is simply a radical ideologue intent upon destroying a government which allowed for enslavement of Black people in the first place, and then, even after granting the Black Man's manumission and subsequent enfranchisement, continued to see him as an inferior being and prejudicially to be regarded so by the non-Black citizenry. However, under a changed or different national ideology the government would be free, setting the Constitution aside, to enact reaching corrective policies long felt needed and anticipated by the Black Man, certainly so by his openly activist leaders. Others of President Obama's following, especially the non-Black ones, might see the pursued change more as a needed upheaval to chasten forever a vaulting, aggrandizing, aggressively competitive individualistic society such as ours, and have it become a more collective, harmonizing society in which all would share resources equally with the government presiding over redistribution of the nation's wealth. It could be seen that the Black Man might embrace just such an agenda to assist him in achieving material parity with his non-Black fellow citizens, a parity which would be *mandated* by government in fulfillment of its ideologic principles. Such an ideology would even admit of such initiatives as "Social Justice," or "Economic Rehabilitation," most felicitous terms which might more passionately be read by activist beneficiaries as Social Revenge and Reparations. Be that as it may, and however just and tactical President Obama may regard such initiatives to be, as well as demanded, we don't believe such is his primary goal. Moreover, we don't think he is an ideologue solely dedicated to a

136

political theory. No, it is likely more a matter of his drawing upon the Socialist/Communist ideology as a convenient, available, and recognized means to his larger end, an end perhaps even shared openly by some of his intimates.

But what is that end? To put it simply, we think President Obama is trying to save his people just as the Prophets of old undertook to save their people. We see that much, if not most of President Obama's legislation, is for assisting the poor, or at least gaining enough control of the economy to force such legislation into law. It is openly but quietly acknowledged that the term, "the poor," is a cledonism for the Black community in America, and most specifically those members of the Black community who can't take care of themselves in an advanced, scientific, technologic society as is America's; the ones who, despite aggressive affirmative encouragement and opportunity shaped to their need, are still unable to see such given preference as other than a means of securing continued government assistance and subsidy rather than as an assist in gaining financial independence of the government through individual and sustaining enterprise geared to their becoming more a part of mainstream America. No, government financial assistance and preferment are not widely used by the Black Man as a means to independent financial and occupational status, but are embraced by too many as an entitled compensation in itself with the result that he never rises above custodial status, and thus continues as a fixed ward of the government, his new master. As a "community organizer" President Obama was vigorous in directing his people to the existence and availability of government assistance and subsidy such that vast use was made of the government's rôle as caretaker of the individual, thereby richly contributing to that regrettable reversal of the people-government dyad: the government was now to direct and oversee the *people* rather than the people direct and oversee the *government*. Plus, the Black Man's long-developing identity transition from having the individual White slave owner as his master to having the government his new master very likely adumbrated the general workability, exploited by the President, of an administrative tactic and strategy which undertakes by legislative stroke to have both the Black Man *and* the White Man functionally co-equal in dependency as well as in means with each subject as well beholden to a defining, regulating, and subsidizing government. In the overall, individual differences, capacities, and reach are to be submerged in a system where reward is provided by governmental schedule, not individual enterprise. The individual and his distinguishing givens are now disenfranchised as such and his identity is now homogenized into a regulated, collectivized citizenry. In effect, the Black Man, by fiat, has now caught up, at least as long as individual differences and capacities are not permitted their run. Equality is proclaimed, along with unanimity. Needless to say, the Constitution, which espouses individual freedom and liberty, would have to be set aside along with traditional notions of private ownership. Not to do so would perversely support the evolution of more adaptive and successful *individual* approaches to the demands of life. And racial differences would soon again appear and exert their effect.

This is the political ideology President Obama has enlisted as his format in correcting imbalances between Black and non-Black societies in this nation. Since the Black Man, as a race, seems unable *sui generis* to move beyond his present level of cultural, social, and industrial accomplishment while non-Black society moves on rapidly and widens the gap, the only ameliorative to this predicament is for the non-Black society to take a step backwards and join with the Black Man as citizens of a communal society directed by government policy with every citizen and his lot being defined socially, economically, and politically in accordance with statute. All citizens would then be legislated as functionally equal in social status as well as political signification, and tendencies toward differentiation would be checked by disapprobation as well as by official proscription. And an ideal Socialism/Communism would be achieved.

Such an accomplishment would redress the vast culture and capacity difference between the Black and the non-Black worlds in our society, and a programmed overall equality of status and means would apply to each citizen. Racial differences as might be amplified by unbound individual endeavor would be removed and a common man, committed to the social, industrial, and economic compass of the government, would evolve. And a new kind of social Justice and economic Equality would have been achieved. President Obama would then have a singular personal as well as ideologic triumph to his credit. As estimable as that triumph would be we still don't think such is his actual goal. A means? Yes, albeit a means which flies in the face of inexorable and determinative natural selection, but, even so, still and all not his goal.

And what might that goal be? Nothing less than salvation of the Black race, its deliverance to begin right here in America.

Many people covertly suspect, but are careful not to express openly, that the Black race, as a race, will never of its own catch up with the other races of the world. The Black race is simply too far behind what with its never having achieved an alphabet much less the art of writing, even pictographic writing. Its art is largely primitive and more illustrative. The metaphysics of meaning is not part of its palette. The typical Black Man's speech, with its touch of the phatic, often carries a distinctive enunciation which is rooted in speech-center Neurology along with the accompanying Anatomy of the speech organs, and is very likely a *genetically* determined trait easy enough to demonstrate though no one seems to want to do so, and likely because of the social and political tremors as would come. President Obama's own enunciation style demonstrates the point even though he was reared in an almost exclusively White setting. Plus, the wheel was unknown to many parts of sub-Sahara Africa, and cannibalism was a tribal practice until quite recently and likely is still practiced in the more remote Black areas of Melanesia. The evolutionary time differences separating the Black race from the White and Oriental races is likely in the neighborhood of many tens

of thousands of years, given the slow pace of neurologic and ana-
tomic change in the hominid sub-specie set. Even then, if given that
amount of additional time, the Black race might still not change
along distinctive White or Oriental lines, but pursue on entirely
different phenotype such that cultural development would not
approach parity ever. Countless generations of cocker spaniels would
likely not result in a golden retriever, or even a generic dog.
Miscegenation would seem the only hope in such a pursuit, but that
in itself would mean the end of the Black race as such.

Truly, it is the degree of Culture Capital which seems to relate
positively to a society's ability to take care of its own needs. The
Black community has precious little Culture Capital of its own in as
much as it relies so heavily on non-Black societal achievement which
Black society seems yet unable to duplicate on its own. This state of
affairs is exemplified in the repeated rescue efforts mounted by non-
Black society in succor of the inhabitants of Black nations which are
unable to look after the needs of their own people in the face of social
and environmental calamities which befall them. But such humanitarian help is often also needed even in more pacific times.

All and all, much of the Black race is close to becoming the
ward of the more advanced nations of the world, and the same applies
to a large segment of the Black race in this country who similarly and
illustratively rely on various government subsidies specifically designed to offset the otherwise inevitable economic and industrial
imbalances existing between the Black and the White communities.
Hence, the Black community is at risk in just those ways which bear
on race survival. It can be said that it's not the spotted owl which is
the endangered species, but the Black race itself, and the many
Black-oriented government programs and subsidies tacitly but clearly
point to this concern. The overall relatively meager return on such
initiatives is strongly suggestive that the Black Man, unlike the
Orientals, has "topped off" in what he can access of American
cultural and industrial largesse (see Entry X). The inexorable forces
of progressive natural selection applying in the educational,

industrial, and economic sectors of non-Black society underscore that trend emphatically. Some of the more vehement activist Black leaders are quite cognizant of this point.

It is this grievous inevitability President Obama wishes to belay, though its time frame is not in administrations, decades, or generations, but likely in tens of thousands of years. It took Neanderthal fifteen thousand years to be replaced by Cro-Magnon, and miscegenation was apparently not an available option to slow the progression along. Still and all President Obama appears to want non-Black America to forfeit more of its gains in favor of providing the Black race with more means as would enhance its survivability, reduce its alienation, blunt the effect of unbridled natural selection, and secure a certain safety come of being materially on par with non-Blacks. Plus, it appears he intends to achieve such not only at home, but *abroad* as well. In a word he wants to save the Black race from Darwinian extinction as would assuredly come over time. And he is thusly a Messiah, at one with his mission, and seemingly unconcerned with the damage imposed on the productive, innovative, and *sustaining* non-Black community in his effort to impose a comprehensive, legislated equality of all. Or at least the ordained appearance of such.

08 April 2010

XX

Love Thy Neighbor

In most of the Western World the Biblical imperative that one love his neighbor is seen as divine guidance and a fundamental component of one's duty for achieving deliverance into the Kingdom of Heaven. It may even be said that this commandment is the seminal tenet whereby Christianity alone, among the major religions of the world, preaches the brotherhood of man. Others may recommend compassion, or advise tolerance, though some actually call for the shunning of all other faiths. Also, it is known that at least one religion adjures the faithful to kill infidels. Even Barbarism is not without its guiding principles, it seems. Plus, there is an ancient Oriental proverb which advises one to shun the unfortunate, regardless of his faith. But Judeo-Christian lore is rich in accents of the precept that all men are to be seen as creations of God and hence not only equal in divine reckoning but brothers in the way of God's will. The godly way is thus also the path of brotherly love for thy neighbor, be he fortunate or not.

Implied in the teachings of this imperative is also the duty of helping one's neighbors in their time of need. The Good Samaritan readily comes to mind in contradistinction to the admonishments of that dismissive, pitiless Oriental proverb which advises otherwise. In Judeo-Christian teachings a godly people should not only love and help needy neighbors, but do so even if they are of a different tribe, faith, or race, inasmuch as they are thy neighbors still. Kind acts of charity, compassion, even self-sacrifice are basic to the ministry of Christianity, and for centuries minions of the faithful have traveled far and wide to help others, particularly the benighted, and, pari passu, have taught the Lord's blessings to peoples of many lands. This faith and its mission have lent their stamp to our national initiatives in the dispensing of aid and succor to beset nations needy beyond their capacity and ability to manage the vicissitudes and urgencies of their lot in life. In this regard whatever else may be said of America, its legacy has always been one of generous assistance to peoples of greatest need, and especially neighbors sore beset by cataclysmic misfortune. Moreover, such assistance has been on a scale immeasurably more bountiful than that ever offered by other contributing nations, often themselves recipients of such aid at some earlier time.

But this nation's documented largess and generosity carry an attendant question. Simply, the question arises as to what form and quantity such assistance should take, especially in the case of any needy neighbor adjudged wanting by comparison with the productivity and capacity of its generous and much more developed neighbor. Ideally, such assistance should be just that amount and sort as would help the needy neighbor enjoy social, cultural, and industrial benefit preliminary to and supportive of his "own" initiative for moving on to domestic independence and self-sufficiency, perhaps even to become at some point along the way a contributor to the assistance of needy others of whatever faith, tribe, or race.

But given the commendable and inspiring thrust of such a goal several ineluctable challenges stand available to thwart the better purpose intended, at least as it applies domestically here in America. Two such challenges may be cited now. Both have been addressed elsewhere, but only in their derivative forms, not in their more basic reference.

The first of these is the heritage of Slavery. Here the imperative to love thy neighbor had no application of any substance. In antebellum America the Black man was property, emancipated or not. He was regarded as essentially a labor apparatus requiring proprietary management and direction. He was seen as having no ennobling goals of his own, and his only purpose was that assigned him by his manager-owners. After emancipation the Black man's status changed only marginally; he was still seen as an apparatus but now

144

a cast-off left to his own devises which reached little beyond his achieving mere survival. But, since society could then no longer use him as before, society no longer bothered to concern itself with his needs. He became an aberrant, peripheral element of the citizenry, the more marginalized the better, and, whatever his place, inveterately seen everywhere as the White man's burden.

The Black man's social and political status began to change favorably some fifty years ago. But now, today, even after a half century of remediation and realignment of the larger society's conception of itself along with its values, including the Black man's status in the socio-political milieu, the grim legacy of Slavery continues, and it does so in large part because its wounds have been opportunistically institutionalized to become politically profitable devices for transmuting an historical injustice—an effect—into a current partisan force—a cause—which seeks compensation and amends by way of legislated preferment for Blacks—who were never slaves—in the form of reparation from Whites—who were never slave owners—even though such frank political opportunism demonstrably exerts a *paradoxical* drag effect on the Black man's better efforts at achieving functional social parity and economic self-sufficiency in America today.

But just what is it in that existential mix which holds the Black man back? More obliquely, what is it about White society which binds it to the support of social and political indemnities, which, despite their want of lasting effectiveness, are offered to the Black man as protectives from the normal and expectable vicissitudes of ordinary commerce in the larger society? These protectives, such as Affirmative Action, are indulgences and advantages not extended to other races or ethnic groups in the American population and hence are morally, perhaps even legally, suspect, at least from the standpoint of fairness and common sense.

White guilt is the conventional answer and indeed does cover much of the issue. It also shapes most of the rhetoric flavoring the matter. Because of the legacy of slavery national guilt is indeed in order, but the current White citizenry is blameless, except by racial consanguinity, of the evils practiced by their forbears of two centuries ago. Nevertheless, White America of today stands accused of those evils and the charges carry an immediacy about them demanding redress by those guilty only of that consanguinity. Actual innocence of the past, and extending over the several subsequent generations, seems not to matter in redressing the great wrong of historical Slavery, nor in assuaging the sustained suffering said to come of it. Is this because Slavery's malevolent wrong-doing, in some altered form, continues to happen? Actually, such appears *not* to be the case.

But, then, what *is* the case? Lamentably, it appears to be a pall come of the second challenge which is the Black man's fixed and collective societal and cultural shortfall, a wretched racial fact which is also the most fiercely tabooed verity relevant to the discussion at hand. To wit, the Black man, because of his cultural and societal shortfall remains disadvantaged vis-à-vis his more advanced neighbors of other races whether he has a history of Slavery or not. See Africa of today. The Romans, a militaristic, regimented republic, conquered Greece, in large part a loose collection of artistic and academic city-states, and subsequently began a slave trade in Greeks to supplement Rome's workforce. However, the Greeks, socially and culturally superior to the Romans, soon became the teachers and artists of their captors. Loot indeed. As the Romans relaxed bondage of the Greeks the latter went on to their former pursuits essentially unchanged, save for being perhaps a bit wiser about the value of Spartan military organization. They did not remain emancipated slaves living out a crippling social and cultural blow inflicted on their kind; they simply put aside the yoke of Slavery and went back to being miraculous Greeks. In a word, they had better things to do, and went ahead and did them.

So where did the Blacks go upon emancipation? Closer to where they were before, just like the Greeks, but in the case of the Blacks, more to a tribal existence. See inner city America.

146

To explore the issue more fully one must reach beyond the boundaries of what is today seen as political correctness, itself a provided indemnity: to wit, uncomplimentary observations, however valid, are not to be allowed in the case of the Black man. Nor is his accountability to the validity of such observations allowed. But beyond that, even simple objectivity of comparison is held suspicious, or handily discounted, in any attempt to trace out important particulars relevant to the point. Blackness is just not to be seen at all, though White, Yellow, and Red are allowed. Thus a certain poignancy threatens to season the inquiry and, of itself, tends to underscore the sore intent of those indemnities.

For example, it is well known but suitably ignored that the Black race and its separate cultures have not achieved an enviable record in keeping pace with the other races and cultures of the world. On the larger scale of it, entire nations and regions in the Black world have repeatedly come to depend on the more advanced and developed nations of the world for assistance in addressing the effects of some calamity or other striking the Black world, calamities man-made or natural. Those Black societies simply have not been able to generate within their social, industrial, and economic structure the resources and safeguards as would service societal needs during such straitened times. Those calamities, such as drought or war, typically see the dissolution of central governmental control with societal reversion to a tribal existence, sometimes even to an even more regressed state. As well in times unmarked by such calamities, Black nations often find themselves in need of First World agencies for assistance in maintaining a civilized posture, much less the social services supportive of a responsible citizenry. It is yet to be recorded that a Black nation has come to the neighborly and generous support of a calamitously stressed White or Oriental nation or culture. Nor to even some other Black nation. Nor does it seem soon to happen. In a word, Black nations and cultures appear quite fully and chronically beset with the task of adequately maintaining their own social, cultural and industrial integrity for addressing even the ordinary demands of civilized society.

Given that lamentable and enduring state of affairs, why is it that Black societies, so often in need of such succor from other racial and national groups, generally don't count the assistance, often as it is on a global scale, as worthy of acknowledged gratitude, or even of simple recognition? How often does one hear of Black leaders, especially those immediately organic to their desperate and needy following, speaking their gratitude to their helpful neighbors, usually predominantly White, who have stepped forth to assist and protect those leaders' endangered peoples? Seldom, even though such assistance may, and has, taken the form of countless tons of food to feed the starving, or, often enough, legions of medical missionaries to stave off the spread of disease. Could it be that those embattled Black societies see such assistance as simply expectable, a justified entitlement come of their low status in the human cultural line-up? Could it be that those societies see such support and protection as not only deserved but also as rightful issue come of the collective duty of Man, and do so even up to the point of justifying their resentment when such help is not very immediately forthcoming? Could their grievous need, so often and tellingly beyond their capacity to address on their own, carry in its very nature the seeds of a resentful envy of those societies which, in their cultural and economic advantage, step forth to help, their enabling wealth and generosity courting indictment because of the "unfair" difference in estate? Worse, does an endangered, disadvantaged society, brought to global recognition as failing in its ability to sustain itself among the more functional societies of the world, automatically label its plight as the fault of others, not of itself? This too often seems so. But, if so, it thus seems to touch upon something primitive in the human psyche which holds that, despite differences in wherewithal and capacity, those who have more morally "owe" a measure of their wealth to those who have less and who are sorely beset for the lack of it. This notion finds its apotheosis fully embraced by the Christian canon of Charity, the essential point of which is that Charity is something freely provided, not demanded, legislated, or appropriated. Such would not be Charity. It is fundamentally an individual act of generosity and compassion; a recognition of the disadvantaged status, whatever the cause, of another who cannot provide for himself that which is needed. In effect, a moral and personal issue even if on a national scale; not an economic or political issue even if on a racial scale.

And that may be a large part of the problem.

So, acceptance of succor and assistance, especially on a national or societal, and especially on a racial scale, conveys open recognition of the recipient's need for others to step forth and assume some measure of caretaking of that recipient, whether temporarily or as standard and continuing policy. It is also open recognition of the recipient's failure, whatever the cause, to provide for himself or his kind. Thus, to many, charity and compassion may carry an oblique indictment of the recipient's failure to repair in managing the urgencies and necessaries of life as they may come. The recipient is operationally seen as adaptationally inferior to his benefactors, and this may well be a darkly unwelcome aspect of the delivered assistance. This is a common theme among welfare recipients. When experienced on a national, societal, or racial scale by the recipient, such help, however sincerely intended, might thus also be seen by the recipient as disingenuous, lordly, and even cynical on the part of the giver who too often is automatically and defensively seen as part, if not the entire cause, of the problem in the first place. And help may thus be resented, though needed. So it would come as no surprise that the recipients would shade any gratitude or obligation on their part into a much lessened recognition of the caring and compassion intended by the giver. And perhaps inevitably so. After all, do a man a favor and etc, etc. But the problem is more accurately and appropriately to be seen as that of the recipient, not of the giver, and the inability to see such—in effect, an inability to look at oneself objectively and honestly, and more to come on that point later—is perhaps not at all oblique to the generative capacity of the recipient's society. A seminal vulnerability, so to speak. Yet, it can be quite politic to see the problem as deriving of the giver as having something extra to give in the first place: after all, a primarily more "equitable" distribution of goods would prevent from the outset such an unfair localization of excess, wouldn't it? Entire political systems are based on the effort to avoid the reality and consequence of individual differences, and all manner of conceptual legerdemain and economic jugglery are employed to offset the inevitable and immutable play of natural selection, be it on the individual, national, or racial scale. But each such system is ideologically and inevitably at odds with the human creative spirit which inheres, not in the horde or its collective needs, but in the nous of the individual.

In a kindred and institutionalized way this issue is what daily confronts the entire world, not only America. As said, it is clear that American Black society has not achieved, much less sustained, parity with its fellow White and Oriental citizens, and that a large portion of Black American society is a chronic recipient of government welfare assistance, even to the point of that group's constituting a custodial class which will remain so for the foreseeable future. It has been suggested that the Black man's having "topped off" in assimilating the skills and practices come of his having been introduced—albeit initially as slaves—to civilized White American society has lamentably left a large portion of his fellow Black American citizens shy still of those industrial and technologic skills as would support his reach for societal parity, unavoidable innate differences in personal capacity presiding (See Entry XVIII). This tragic circumstance serves as a remorseless gnomen to the general non-Black American populace as well as to the world at large in its efforts to sustain an optimism in support of the custodial effort. Legislation continues to feature various assistance and preferences granted "the Poor," all of it funded disproportionately by the non-Black sector of taxpayers. The programs are through and through charitable initiatives the non-Black taxpayers see as intended for unfortunate others, almost all exclusively members of "minorities" and "the Poor." The programs

150

even undertake to feed the children of those recipients in an attempt to encourage and fortify a sense of parental responsibility and adequacy. And the general, tax-paying citizenry is generally sympathetic and supportive of such legislation inasmuch as the recipients have nowhere else to turn, given their cultural shortcomings, shortcomings which have not, as stated earlier, been adequately effaced by long exposure to the cultural and societal endeavor of their fellow citizens. But however the extent of compassion and hope carried by such assistance and support, its chronicity works a corrosive effect upon the dignity and self-respect of the recipient and his kind. In time, the chronicity of the gesture seems to turn the gesture rancid to the recipient who, offended by the continuing programmatic display of his inferior social and economic status in the larger society, soon mounts a defensive, self-serving stance vis-à-vis the assistance: the aid and preferment are now in no wise to be seen as addressing Black inadequacy but rather a just entitlement come of crippling crimes inflicted by White society. In this sense the social scene in America sees frank parallel with sub-Sahara Africa and its quarrel with historical Colonialism. The "Poor" in America, numbering close to forty millions, constitute a Third World nation in culture and societal style living within and supported by a First World nation with the attendant chronic political draw upon the latter to yield more of its largesse to the needier former, just as with sub-Sahara nations and their relation to the more advanced nations of the world, especially in times of crisis in the former.

Hence, the durable value of historical slavery, or colonialism, in the salving of any spuriously justified reach for current remediation or wealth redistribution. With such a self-serving perspective, the recipient may now justifiably feel bitterness, entitlement, and open militancy in the face of his having been placed unfairly in such a wretched state, erstwhile as a slave and now as the deprived "Poor." Hence, the more assistance required and granted, the more anger and vengefulness stoked for having been reduced so; and the more social programs of remediation exacted, the more vengeful the pursuit of a corrective justice. Needless to say, a political ideology exploitative of just such a canted maneuver in "self-esteem" acquisition would soon enough and inevitably make its presence known, and would of course be exquisitely contrapuntal to the notion of personal freedom in the service of life, liberty, the pursuit of happiness—*and* individual responsibility. Plus, it would be dedicated to a most tendentious way of defining empirical Truth, if it bothered with Truth at all. Certainly it would depend heavily upon a society's gracious readiness to love beset neighbors who necessarily and vengefully exempt themselves of any reciprocation or even gratitude as a just and more civil means of feeling good about themselves.

22 November 2010

XXI

Win-Win, Sort Of

It has been stated in earlier installments (see Entries III, IV, V, et al) that President Obama does not have the best interests of America *qua* America at heart. It was speculated that he sees this nation, its founding documents, its governmental structure, its societal format, certainly its economic credo as part and parcel a fundamentally White Racist society despite its manifesto of equality of all under the law. True, the persistence of seemingly intractable and unyielding racial differences in the sweep of human endeavor and the fruits deriving therefrom sees its grim playing out in the warp and weft of this nation's popular fabric despite a national overlay of opportunity and promise as exists nowhere else in the world. And, verily, it's been said, if all too bluntly, that if you can't make it in America, you simply can't make it. Plus, the reasons cited for the disparity in racial weal continue to cover all manner of identifiable influences, local and convenient ones generally being the more featured. In America, the historical fact of slavery is the standard and favored one, with racial prejudice running a close second hard in its wake.

Moreover, it is typically held by the endorsers of such thinking that Slavery inflicted a crippling and enduring wound on all of America, and that the evil of that deed continues in force today as nationalized Racism, whether manifest or latent. The fact that the Black man was indeed enslaved affixes to White America the stamp of Racist as much as it affixes to Black America the stamp of Benighted. And no escape from these stigmata seems possible. Plus, not only does such seem to be the accepted view of Black America but also that of the majority of White America as well. And respondent behaviors flow accordingly, seldom departing from the set-piece dyad of Murderers and their Victims constantly seeking each other, as Plato is supposed to have viewed humanity.

It is clear that President Obama, and notably some less circumspect members of his Cabinet, embrace this perspective vigorously. Pronouncements such as "my people," referring to Black citizens, and "our time has come," certainly referring to an expected change in race ascendency, are heard, and, perhaps not oddly, go unchallenged by the larger citizenry in keeping with a collective and invidious script commanding all to play out the presumed harmatia of the American predicament.

President Obama has certainly seized upon this absorption as his mandate to draw the curtain on a guilty America; and the general electorate—variously shaded in contrition, retribution, guilt, fear—seems mesmerized into a mode of resignation where once a capacity for bold outrage held sway. Some, but not enough, still hold that America *qua* America, warts and all, is to be protected and preserved as the mainstay of a hopeful world not yet open, free, or brave enough to question its own basic assumptions as America asks of itself, and does.

It is specifically because of President Obama's unyielding enmity toward the America of the daily citizen that his agenda is more and more manifestly one of changing this nation into a communal enterprise in which reckoning of personal worth is no longer left to the energies and talents of the individual but rather to the by-laws of mandated governmental address. By all manner of measure the Black race has been culturally a consistent under-achiever in the world of civilized endeavor and has thus experienced the consequence of carrying custodial status in much of its interface with the other races of the world. President Obama's campaign of Hope and Change bears most specifically on this predicament though it was astutely left non-specific in the electoral campaign's telling of its particulars to allow the general populace enough room for ranging application across the spectrum of common discontent, need and fancy. However, the Black electorate knew exactly what he meant.

154

To accomplish the change he sought, President Obama favored a format based on distribution of commodities in accordance with centralized levy, not one based on individual productivity. In the latter format the great leveler and the "fair and equal" starting point in the production and consumption of commodities is personal freedom, freedom within collectively agreed upon guidelines in applying ones energies and talents for the securing of commodities along with the right to dispose of those commodities as one wished. Such personal freedom is to be enjoyed and observed equally under the law. This format, called free enterprise, presumes an open market for the observance and practice of such freedom.

In the former format, centralized levy, personal freedom is not a key element. Personal *need* is. The great leveler here is demonstrable and measurable personal need. Commensurate satisfaction of need is the ideal, and thus specification of personal need then becomes the "fair" starting point in the production and consumption of commodities. With programmatic satisfaction of *need* being foremost, control of production becomes the paramount method of addressing such need equitably. This approach—central control as determinative of production—is antithetical to the contrasting approach—personal freedom as the engine of production—and results in a fundamental difference in market share designation. The personal freedom approach leads to a free market with commodity distribution being determined by *supply* and *demand*. The control production approach forbids a free market, and commodity distribution is determined by adjudicated *need*. Those who need more get more, regardless of who produced what. But in the personal freedom approach those who produce more *have* more, and therefore have more to contribute to the general market for its address of supply and demand. Thus, in the control production approach individual pursuit is not allowed to result in an imbalance of distribution come of personal ability and enterprise; rather, individual productivity is to be coordinated with group need, and group need is to be assessed according to its political relevance. In effect, enterprise is to be harnessed to political goals, and individual self-interest, along with the prospect of personal gain, is accordingly subordinated to the maintenance of regulated commodity distribution. Individual, and, ultimately, even racial differences in productivity and profit are programmatically set aside as major considerations in the economic forces pacing communal growth; rather, centralized directive now serves as the definer and director of economic focus. *Neediness* now ceases to be an oblique measure of failed personal or group adaptability but is now a *standardized* variable to be included in the formation of economic policy. In effect, people are required to be needy for there to be policy at all. A general sharing of life style would be pursued, and *need,* not freedom, would become the great leveler, programmatically experienced by all and, ideally, experienced equally. Government would orient itself to the pursuit and equilibration of popular need, not to individual or group success in having per force *obviated* need by dint of enterprise's yield. Thus, the slogan: from each according to his ability, to each *according to his need*, a forbysen which establishes *need* as the imprimatur of responsible citizenship. Thus a good citizen is one who *needs* his government as opposed to the citizen who simply *supports* his government, the question of who is serving whom being adjusted accordingly. One cannot emphasize this point too much. Also, one need not look far to identify those citizens to whom this format would appeal. Thus, the economic strategy of one format—the one embracing freedom—undertakes to erase need, while the other—the one embracing central levy and control—undertakes to standardize need as the gnomen for distribution of commodities. Hence, two very different personal and social realities: the one, open and expectant; the other, regulated and prescribed. The one identifies largesse as the beacon of the future; the other establishes need as the certification of responsible, even patriotic, citizenship. Each adumbrates a vastly different conception of life.

But could the central levy format, equalizing the lot of all, ever square with natural law and the rules of Nature which flatly give us winners and losers? Of course not, but, as an ameliorative to soften a social "unfairness" come of the free and impersonal playing out of individual and group destinies, it promises a political utility, even if merely in the short run and usually only after innate and inevitable social irreconcilables become so wretchedly overbearing and obvious in their effect that a corrective counter-stroke seems desirable but which, in its application, suspends Natural law in favor of a political and tendentious adjustment of the societal landscape. One would think that the arch Environmentalists, so given as they are to the preservation of a natural, untampered surround would eschew such frank social engineering, but they don't, and perhaps in part because their policies implicitly but necessarily exempt themselves of obedience to it. But, nevertheless and in due time, the forces and benefits of creative individuality soon re-assert themselves and the playing out of contending and contrasting destinies and their social and cultural inevitabilities starts all over again.

Hence, there is built-in poignancy with President Obama's agenda. It cannot really change any of the human fundamentals which give us the America of today. Nor can it erase or efface those individual givens which designate position in the collective adaptation-success line-up. As well it cannot forbid those givens from collecting into more obviously recognizable racial or even ethnic groupings. Whatever the intent of his agenda and its social goals, it will not homogenize its recipients into a blameless, unbiased, equal mix. Individual differences and their normal distribution will persevere and their driving force for expression will not abate. And in that relentless process there will be definite winners, definite losers, and many, many also-rans, whatever the challenge may be.

Hence, one need not wonder that in the collective human dynamic there is the civilization-driven and periodic need of respite from the relentless march of natural individuation and its derivative structuralization of society. We in our lifetime and especially over the past twenty years have seen the technology explosion bring amplification of difference between those who can harness and utilize its potential benefits and those who cannot. Those who can are racing on to a new level of adaptational address of the environment, and those who earlier were marginal participants in the human array are now falling even farther below the mean because of their sorely limited capacity to embrace developmentally that very technology. It is long known that no new discovery elevates all equally, and it is just as well known that every new discovery divides the sample into leaders and followers. It is perhaps this ruthless re-ordering, or the unsparing extension of pre-existing societal layerings, which periodically calls for respite from the consequential ongoing socio-political tensions come of bright, new departures made available for some but only a settled fixity of status for others, such respite usually taking the form of a political ideology designed to blunt temporarily the social individuation and layering-out process inevitably come of natural selection. Also, such respite usually favors an unrealistic yet demonstrably more merciful reach for social homogeneity, and all in the name of civilized social husbandry. More on that to come.

But for now we are adequately employed in discerning the personal stakes President Obama assigns to his agenda, derived as it is of his racial identification and the general plight of his kind. As stated earlier President Obama hates America as White racist from its very inception and throughout its history. It is also clear he intends to elevate the Black man at least to parity. Along with that pursuit he intends to punish White America for its sins against the Black race as well as for its proud exceptionalism. His weapon clearly is a political ideology which eschews individual enterprise while empowering centralized distribution of commodities—"spread the wealth," as he has said. Thus, the very political structure of the nation is to be changed, and, thus, founding documents are to be set aside in favor of a new ideology. In effect, historical America is to be dismantled and a new, more Socialist America is to be founded. The old order is to be retired. Therein lie the stakes President Obama brings to his task, and therein lie the win-win prospects of his effort. It is unlikely he could establish the new order without first destroying the old.

Thus, the deed of having the new order functionally in place would connote and actually comprise victory in the utmost. But even if the new order cannot be instituted in its totality—in effect, only a limited victory—the old order will have been abridged to an equal extent, and the resultant damage inflicted on traditional White America would, to him, be an accomplishment in its own right. Any measure of legislated change in accordance with his agenda would be registered as a successful stroke against the America he coldly loathes. And even if his every effort fails and America remains largely unchanged, he will still be successful for having garnered this nation's highest office, formerly the seat of White America's noblest and keenest advocates, and having perverted it into a means of destroying what it was meant to serve—the advocacy of all of America—but now the seat of Black hatred of White America.

In effect, a win-win situation for him, sort of, but one which raises great concern in the minds of many as to how he can possibly regard himself a genuine American, if at all he does.

03 April 2011

XXII

The Pits and the Pendulum

The previous entry made reference to the historical record's display of civilized man's attempts at representative government and how the results seem to oscillate between two antithetical nodal points on the basis of the individual's adaptational capacity and his assigned and recognized rôle in the civic structure of his society. Recent history has portrayed the contrasting ideologies with Hegelian starkness such that the contrast seems established as one more enduring duality to be logged in among the many bedeviling the human predicament. To review, it was noted that the two antithetical political ideologies arose largely in reaction to the excesses and evils of each come of the logical and inevitable reduction to extremity of the other in the playing out of their innate destinies. In that regard it also seems established that neither of the two ideologies, in their growth and decline cycles, lasts very long, giving rise to the expectable phenomenon that the bulk of the civilized world seems ever poised to discern some tempering and sobering trend each ideology may have upon the other in playing out more enduringly some reconciled destiny. To wit, Alexander Tytler, Lord Woodhouselee, introduced here in an earlier installment (see Entry XI), has detailed the stages in the life cycle of Democracies, and it is clearly within our recent experience to note that Communist Democracies are no less doomed by their own inner workings than are Capitalist Democracies, the doctrinal fatalities of each ideology coming of and bearing the telling and finely articulated signature of extremity latent in their founding credos, or, as Hegel might say, the antithesis latent in any thesis.

Let's take Tytler's *stages* of Democracy as our starting point. In its standard rendering, the sequence of stages would ideally see its application in a democratic society notably homogeneous along the usual line of social attributes—language, religion, race, customs, etc. Tytler holds that Democracies begin as movements energized and directed by inspirational pursuits, usually identified with or closely allied to religious underpinnings. That may well and does seem to be the case, but it can be asked if such applies not only to Democracies. To sharpen our reference in broader address of this question it may be useful for us to review the stages of a given Democracy's growth and decline as set down by Tytler. The stages are:

From bondage to spiritual faith

This stage is usually begun by some spark igniting a long-kindling despair or deprivation in which hope for the citizen's plight is in grave danger of being irrevocably extinguished, or is felt to be so. A messianic figure, an inspirational text, or even some grave worsening of the societal lot, such as a disastrous war, or a famine, can supply that spark which illuminates in the collective thinking of a subject people the way to a new horizon.

From spiritual faith to great courage

The new horizon, whose time seems to have come and is thus undeniable, is galvanized by the standing despair which now calls for courage in rejecting the old social order in favor of the adventure-some new. It is usually at this time, if not accomplished earlier, that some charismatic figure is identified, and a rough delineation of leaders and followers, revolutionaries and reactionaries, is made.

From courage to liberty

Activated revolution is the key turning point at this time, and will take its tactical stamp from the oppressive aspects of the existing social setting which incites it. Plus, this setting may have determinative components as to the subsequent disposition of power in the pursuit of revolutionary goals. For example both Czarist Russia and Colonial America experienced revolutions of liberation, each claiming Liberty to be the desideratum with each announcing itself an achieved representative Democracy. But important differences applied and these differences defined vastly different paths of political and social development though each was pursued in the name of Democracy. The Russian people, mostly muzhiks, revolted against an autocracy which had long denied them any rights or any property to speak of. They themselves were property. The Czar had unquestioned power of life and death over them, and such was how their world was defined. The Americans, mostly farmers, revolted against a Monarchy which had violated granted rights already in practice, and defense of those rights and also of private property saw a revolution which preserved much of what already was, save a change in central authority. With the muzhiks, who owned nothing and were themselves chattel, all goods belonged to the Czar and his nobles. Private ownership, at least by simple citizens, was a nebulous concept alien to the world and histories of the Czars. Protection of private property was a notion of little moment in the mind of peasant Russia. Property, its management and control, was hence at the very onset of the new Bolshevik Democracy a keenly regarded matter. Though no longer of and by the Czar and his nobles, property and its management was now to be defined and effected by appointed representatives of the people by way of elections established for that purpose. Plus, control of production was more the matter, not individual freedom in the pursuit of production. This difference sees the beginning of contention between the ideologies of the two systems come of revolution—central control of the collective for production and its distribution, i.e., Communism; and individual enterprise in concert with a free market for production and distribution of its commodities, i.e., Capitalism.

From liberty to abundance

It is at this point that the functional playing out of the separate ideologies begins to appear by way of consequent life style and the well-being of their adherents. It is also the point at which the two populations manifest the personal societal expectancies to come of the particular type of freedom embraced by their separate revolutionary fervors. The muzhik wants to be free in that he doesn't want to be the property of a noble; he wants rights by which he can have some say in the management of his daily existence. The colonial American, however, is already quite free and long has known the right of decision in seeking his place in society; he does not want that right abridged in any way, nor his means of exploiting that right hampered. Rather, he wants control of his destiny to be almost solely his. Thus it appears that separate lines of thought along with the *pre-existing extent of cultural development* predetermine what each seeks in the use of revolution; the muzhik doesn't fundamentally object to being managed but it is to be *management by officials freely elected* of the people; the colonial American has little truck with imposed management of any kind, for his interest is in the *preservation and extension* of rights in the exploitation of *personal freedom* and independence. The muzhik seeks independence of the Czar and freedom from ownership of himself by others but, basically, *not* independence of centralized management inasmuch as his level of cultural development requires that he still be managed. The colonial American wishes to be *independent* of a controlling kingdom because his level of cultural development identifies personal freedom and individual enterprise as his inalienable right. The law he is now to obey is to come only of his kind and in support of his way.

From abundance to complacency

It is at this point that the innate potential and the subsequent yield of the separate ideologies, predetermined in large part by the supportive influence of the receiving culture's level of development at the time of their adoption, begin to manifest their quite different destinies. The difference between the two seems to hinge on the difference in commodity abundance and its method of production.

It is a truism that American abundance is, by any measure, extreme in comparison to that of other nations. It is also true that our land is blessed with natural riches readily available for exploitation and development. But so it is also in other lands, though with far less yield to show for it, such as Soviet Russia and certainly sub-Sahara Africa. The latter especially is still largely bereft of a viable, organizing, much less industrially productive, political ideology distinct from primitive tribalism.

Fundamentally, it is the embrace and the type of political ideology joined to its level of cultural development, plus the availability of resources, which position a society for reach into whatever abundance as may be its potential. But what accounts for the difference in yield between societies so primed? For a consideration of this question it is necessary we briefly shift our perspective from formed ideologies to innate human striving. It may be said that all human beings strive for a comfortable and stabilizing homeostatic state of satisfaction labeled differently by different levels of description to include the biologic, the psychologic, the social, and certainly the spiritual. Such, human striving mobilizes resources in the individual as well as collectively in his group. However, it is the individual resource which is the bedrock quantum in point here, whatever its descriptive level of organization within the individual or beyond, and that resource is the individual's unique disposition of his personal energy/psychic structure relationship universally seen in the developmental transformation from the boundless and unformed energy of the child into the steady faculties and shaped talents of the mature individual. Plus, it need not be said that, ultimately, the energy of the group evolves collectively of the separate energies of the individuals comprising that group. Hence, the energy/structure character of the group is innately individual in origin. However, groups have a tendency to form themselves into organized and purposeful pursuits all of their own, and thus they provide *form* for the shaping and focus of the combined energies of the individual members. But where does that *form* come from, its source? Basically, it is drawn likewise from the energies of the individual members; it is not a commodity available to the group *sui generis*. To wit, the

165

members pay for the group's existence and operation with a portion of their own energy which may be seen as rent for their membership in the group. Thus, membership will always carry a personal as well as collective cost. Nothing new here. But what may be considered here is the effect such an arrangement has on creativity and production. Simply put, it can be said that the more energy invested in the form and structure of the group, the less available for personal use, such as for individual creativity and innovation. Or, we might say, the more rules and regulations, the slower the rate of growth and development to more advanced forms. We could even say that the more taxation (rent), the less wealth (energy) for enterprising growth (productivity). But more on that point at another time. For the nonce we will limit ourselves to Tytler's progression of stages in the life of Democracies.

If what has been said above is true, then it may be expected that, all things equal, the more energy invested in and generative of form, structure, and regulation, the less disposable energy for creativity, production, and growth. And this indeed seems to be the case. Consider Soviet Russia and America at parallel stages in their development as free and sovereign nations, making allowances for the different times in history for those events—1775 and 1917—and the types of monarchies at play. Soviet Russia, from its very inception, was framed in the mold of a vast, articulated bureaucracy which extended into every aspect of the citizen's life, and a correspondingly vast amount of national energy and treasure was expended in sustaining and extending that bureaucracy. Its yield of benefit to the citizen, by Czarist standards, was immense. Education, medical care, social service, industrial opportunity all became available as never before. And it was centrally formatted and directed. But the citizen, whose lot was unquestionably improved, had no say-so in government workings, though he was nominally hailed as having so. The citizen's rôle was to produce and sustain the political and governing structure as defined centrally. Change and growth did not derive of citizen reach, motive, or interest; the trend was preferentially that of perfecting central regulation of daily living, and the citizen tended to comply accordingly. Citizen-driven innovation simply had no rôle in the governing process, and the established governing structure became the definer of abundance and purpose, itself the primary and foremost beneficiary of that pursuit. And personal abundance was relegated to secondary status, perhaps still having more to show for itself over that of Czarist times but comparatively meager among other in-dustrialized nations. And the citizen's acceptance of his status was itself regulated. Individual creativity was transmuted into concerted pursuit of centrally defined national goals. And life became leaden. Complacency, usually understood as connoting comfort, was not a primary ingredient of the societal mix, but resignation was. And Soviet Russia, weighed down by itself, ultimately dissolved even more rapidly than it arose. It's very fate exposed it as being not at all the Democracy it hailed itself to be, much less what is commonly understood by the term. Its precipitous collapse was more like that of its earlier autocracy; an autocracy itself, but of a different sort.

But America, so much more what a Democracy is genuinely meant to be, seems now following faithfully Tytler's stages of decline. America's abundance is such that it can easily breed com-placency, as appears just now to be the case. Indeed, a certain com-placency in the face of our downward drift has likely been present for several decades as signs of a collective national degeneracy mounted (see Entry XI). Brave voices have been sounding the tocsin and a measure of the general citizenry is mobilized to confront the downward drift, but most leaders find in the larger common gender a concerted resistance to any effort to halt and reverse the trend. In a word, most of the people seem to accept the decline if they can be complacently comfortable as it happens. Self-interest and preferment seem to prevail, at least in the short run. All seem to know where the decline is headed but a certain acquiescence overrides the citizenry's lament over what awaits. Worse, the nation's political arm now seems specifically geared to the very process of decline as its legislators enact more and more of what appears to be an evolving

167

mosaic of decay, the present administration's stake in this pursuit amply noted earlier (see Entry XXI).

Hence, the stage is liberally set to nourish a growing and futile despair should current efforts to blunt the downward drift of the times fail. If such ensues it will assuredly nourish an apathy come of a settled futility—our own form of resignation—and our Democracy, thus placed in the full receivership of a malevolent contrivance being enacted and now waiting (see Entry XXI) will find itself on the road to serfdom, and to bondage once again, its dissolution achieved.

25 April 2011

XXIII

Learning to Care for the Poor

Over the past fifty-odd years an increasing portion of this nation's socio-political endeavor has been dedicated to elevating the status of what is recognized variously as our society's "Poor," the "Underclass," the "Disadvantaged," etc. This sector of our society has traditionally held the position of being obliquely exempt of the ususal duties of citizenship, such as paying personal income taxes; achieving an enabling level of education; observing the accepted standards of moral and lawful behavior, especially among themselves; even exemption of dutiful identity with the national spirit of patriotic citizenship. This Underclass has been granted recognition as a "culture" unto itself, separate and uniquely different from the mainstream which energizes the national commonweal. This "culture," albeit a rudimentary one, has even developed its own linguistics and dialect in keeping with the speech characteristics of so many of its members. It offers many generic customs and characteristics which separate it from the mainstream within which it exists, and there are pervasive points of seminal difference which give rise to the question as to whether this sub-culture, rather than being a less advanced derivative of the larger, prevailing culture, is actually more a displaced element of a phylogenetically quite different line of human cultural development, but which, of necessity, conforms with and functions within the larger, prevailing, adoptive culture, though displaced as it is from its own parent culture located elsewhere in pursuit of its own separate and materially different path of development. Indeed, it seems that among the more racially distinct elements of the rooted "Poor" and the sub-cultures derived therefrom, however dispersed and separated those sub-cultures are from their primary, root cultures, even for long periods of time, they still seem to mimic more each other in their cultural ethos than they do that of the larger, adoptive group in which they may find themselves. Group assimilation into the larger culture is forfended in like degree as the individual members collect into a cohesive social sub-unit at the expense of individual assimilation into the larger, adoptive group. Birds of a feather, it seems. This notion is perhaps better demonstrated by applying it on the level of the individual. Let us assume that a perfectly average individual from a culture whose population has a consistently documented average I.Q. of 70 is reared in a culture whose population has an average I.Q. of 100. Even allowing for the enriching effect of enculturation within the higher I.Q. culture this individual would be at a disadvantage in availing himself of the various societal accomplishments of the adoptive culture; he simply would not have the capacity to discern the worth and meaning of that culture's accomplishments, much less be able to access such in a personal identification equal to that of his adoptive cohorts. He would perceive their culture in a vastly different and skewed way compatible with his personal cognitive and emotional variance from the mean of the adoptive culture, and he would likely see himself more kindred to that culture's lesser members but perhaps even then without the benefit of the subtle but vital underpinnings come of legacy and heritage available to all of the native members of that culture. But, correspondingly, he might also demonstrate notable skills which exceed those of his adoptive group. For example, it is an established finding that Bushmen consistently achieve performance on the Proteus Maze Test far superior to the average for persons of Western culture who try their hand at that task. But even so, despite the chance occurrence of unique and exceptional traits in the culturally less accomplished adoptee he is likely to be, because of his cognitive and psychological difference, largely unresponsive to much of the variously-faceted achievements of the richer culture. This person would likely moreso draw upon elements of his parent culture, however removed, in establishing a substitute sub-culture phenotypically consanguine with his innate capacities. And such

170

seems to be the case for a large segment of our general population. However, the determinants and ethos of such a sub-culture might also be just too consanguine with what is generally seen in the Underclass of this nation.

It is perhaps this rooted, deeply phylogenetic influence which exercises such a powerful draw on its Underclass members despite the immediate ubiquity of the more advanced cultural influence of the larger society. Classical music offers itself as an example. The draw that such music has on members of the Underclass is proportionately much less than on members of the adoptive culture, above and beyond difference in socio-economic class of the latter. Attend any classical music concert, and note. No one can fault the great masters of classical music for a lack of skill or creativity, but even the more developed music of the sub-culture seldom constitutes a notable portion of classical music's repertoire. The sub-culture simply doesn't yield much of that genre, but it is rich in music drawn from the rhythms and thrust associated with a more primordial musical experience. Indeed, the very popularity of the latter's music speaks to the vestigial animistic inheritance present in all societies, developing as well as advanced. But the difference in draw to those groups responsive to it spells the difference between where developmentally one has long before been and where one has only more recently arrived.

It is this kind of difference played out along the societal landscape which details the cultural underpinnings of ethnic and racial groups comprising the popular mix of this nation, and pari passu, the ethos of its sub-cultures; specifically, those with high Culture Capital as compared to those having lesser Culture Capital, Capital here being defined in much the same way as it might economically in that the more capital one has, the more one has for investment in growth and development. Groups of a relatively impoverished culture, because of their phylogenetically lower state of cultural development, are unalterably obliged to remain respondent to and dependent upon the culturally richer groups for the industrial and scientific advancements generated by those favored groups. True, lesser cultures might readily adopt and access such advancements but only those cultures with adequate Culture Capital will be likely, or be able, to exploit the heuristic potential of such advances for their own expanded productivity. Also true, many lesser cultures now make good and full use of the computer, but only those with adequate Culture Capital have been able to move on to producing one of their own. The level of general societal sophistication necessary to achieve such industrial capacity would perforce derive of that society's cultural underpinnings. Alas, as of this sitting, those so qualifying are distinctly limited in number. Moreover, any addition to that number from the current lesser cultures does not seem likely in the foreseeable future. To compound the problem farther, it is predominantly from such lesser cultures the Underclass of the advanced cultures tends to draw its membership.

It is this grim layering effect, its inevitability and apparent intractability which is so determinative of the political, the social, and certainly the economic fabric of our nation. And just as inevitably, seemingly intractable issues of conflicted community and entrenched social isolation arise.

In 1897 Joseph Conrad published a novella which portrayed with ghastly clarity the grim devoir besetting all civilized humanity. The novella, most regrettably entitled, "The Nigger of the Narcissus," tells the story of a West Indian Black crew member on a merchant shipping sailing from Bombay to London. The Black, James Wait, takes ill with tuberculosis and is laid up, unable to do his part as a member of the crew. His plight arouses the compassion and humanitarian sympathy of several members of the crew, five of whom, at the risk of their own lives and also the safety of the ship, rescue him from his helpless state during a violent storm that threatens to scuttle the ship and drown all. Other members of the crew, the Captain and First Mate in particular, are indifferent to Wait's plight, given as they are to saving the ship and themselves. One member of the crew, a hateful and vengeful malcontent, as alienated as Wait and who holds all of society the cause of his miserable existence, sees only the need to heap scorn and contempt on Wait and anticipate his death with open and undisguised glee. All survive the storm, save Wait who dies of his tuberculosis before reaching port, and, despite commendable effort at proper obsequy, is clumsily buried at sea.

It is said that the story is to be seen as portraying the contending states of community versus isolation, the ship's crew serving as a microcosm of the larger society of man. There is suggestion that even humanitarian motives are ultimately driven by self-interest—a not too surprising revelation in its own right, given the affirmative visibility of such policy—but more importantly that a heightened sensitivity to the sufferings and misfortunes of others can be at odds with the protection and better direction of a society.

The microcosm of the *Narcissus* and its crew reaches out to the societal circumstance of America today. The benighted Wait—isolated, alien, impaired, dependent on the help of others—is the embodiment of the Underclass of our current society, and he, just as it, incites in us our sympathy and compassion. Allowing him to become the mortal victim of his cruel disadvantage is simply not acceptable to the civilized sensitivities of his crew mates. In the story, several of his crew mates, upon realizing his plight, unhesitatingly band together, and cheered on by other crew members, plunge in to the bowels of the writhing ship, work their way through all the wreckage and destruction within and finally locate him, free him, and bring his failing form forth to where he can be cared for. His rescuers then return to their posts to help their fellow crew members keep the ship afloat and ride out the rest of the storm. But as the storm blows itself out, Wait dies of his tuberculosis. He is burred at sea in full and decent, though clumsy, obsequy. The storm now gone, the silence and halcyon calmness of the sea is, in comparison, reflective and solemn. Soon they reach port and are back in a world which knows nothing of their experience, too busy it is with the struggles of life and death of its own particular form.

The story does not recount that after the storm passed any mention was ever made by any regarding the rescuers' decision to help Wait at the expense of keeping up crew strength in a collective effort to save the ship. No question was asked as to why so potentially costly an effort was made to save an otherwise doomed man from drowning. The matter was allowed to rest as merely devoir rightfully done.

And so it seems with us today. The Poor, it has been so often said, will always be with us. However, it perhaps has not been so often said, at least not openly, that the rest of us will always have to take care of them, the kind and quality of that care varying with the level of civilization, the cultural development, and the economic bearing of the caregiver. One could quite cynically suggest that it is not only the pursuit of freedom and opportunity which daily washes up upon our shore so many needy third world immigrants, legal or otherwise. Available Charity may also apply. Our immigration laws and practices are so quaintly archaic in apparent denial of this truism that nowadays hardly anybody, much less the daily bulk of immigrants, gives the official policy any account, much less notice. It would seem that in its bounden duty to protect the interests and safety of this nation the government would smartly apply its authority and power in a concerted effort to seal that breach in our national security and return the decision of societal composition to its lawful citizens. But, then again, we also have such things as needy political parties. And available votes. And a more manifest display of the wicked cynicism hosting our national degeneracy need not be wished.

Beyond the issue of fraudulent, "illegal" enlargement of the Underclass there is the prevailing matter of the ongoing, endemically occurring size of that group in its traditional segment of the American population; specifically, the ones who have long been with us. The question here is not so much one of regulating the number to be rescued—though that aspect of the problem indeed relates to the larger question of group overall rescueability—but rather to the quantity and kind of rescue to be effected. In this consideration cate-

174

goricals and imponderables quickly come into play. For example, enough rescue to obliterate the Underclass entirely by elevating and rehabilitating all of its members to full participation in the social, industrial, and economic mainstream? All? Yes, all, or else there would arise once again the sin of unfairness, discrimination, racism, and assorted other going taboos kept readily at hand for such moments. So how much rescue? In the vernacular of can-do American thinking, the proper reply is: as much rescue as it takes! In the traditional American approach to social problem-solving it is publicly unacceptable to recognize a given social problem as unsolvable by all civilized or known political or scientific means, much less that *only the consequences* of the problem are approachable and likely with only temporizing results at best, the real issue being beyond the hands of man, a measure of resignation thus quite in order along with a chastened view of rescue and its feasibility suitably in place. Such an approach might bear the stamp of honesty and careful judgment which would undoubtedly aid in preventing the squandering of a nation's treasury in promise of full equality and happiness to all, a state which the infinite and cosmic Wisdom of Nature never, in all its eons, saw fit to pursue, and very likely never will. But as we know, in the world of man we have such things as needy political parties. And keenly coveted votes. And also an uncompromising and unforgiving Piper.

As stated, Conrad appears to address the issue of community and solidarity, and does so against the backdrop of compassion and survival. Wait, the only Black aboard, is incapacitated by his tuberculosis and is thus alienated from his more hale crew members from the very outset. The immediate upshot of this predicament is that Wait has no daily participation in the maintenance of the common vessel and comes to depend on his shipmates' sympathy for what identity he might have as an authentic member of the crew, his only social identity of the moment to serve as the tie supporting the compassion and natural humanity which the crew stand available to offer. Such is the nature of shibboleth and natural community.

175

"Belonging" opens the way to community privilege and protection, the specific rites of belonging defined according to community canon: in the case of the *Narcissus*, fulfilling one's rightful duty as a contributing crew member; as an American, fulfilling one's rightful duty as a contributing and supporting citizen. Wait, as with so much of America's Underclass, falls short of these basic tenets of belonging and community. But the analogy tends to break down when we consider that Wait is only one among many contributors, a condition which undoubtedly deepens the pathos of his plight, while our Underclass numbers well into the millions and constitutes a considerable sector of our general population, a bloc so much less personal than was Wait's predicament amidst his crew mates and so much more an institutionalized societal entity. Thus, Underclass alienation is accordingly aggravated, and proportionately so at the cost of the common sympathetic humanity of others. An Underclass of that magnitude is so much less inclined to assimilation and is more given to a defensive cohesiveness come of sub-culture membership, the sub-culture's resulting relationship to the primary culture of which it is a satellite, commensal at best but saprophytic in the main, and, once again, proportionately so to the degree of difference in Culture Capital between the primary and the satellite. Indeed, there have been sub-cultures; i.e., Greek slaves, vis-à-vis Romans, where the difference has been in favor of the subcultures with the prevailing culture reaping large benefits therefrom, Culture Capital being reckoned not only in size, but depth as well. But this is certainly not the case with our own Underclass and its place in the primary American culture. The American Underclass remains essentially custodial and fixedly so. No matter the American, politically driven definition of "Poor," a definition which would embrace a large measure of the well-do-do of other societies, our Underclass seems to carry an established identity which, lately, features policy and principle which in no small way confers a certain solidarity on its membership. Also, in no small part, this identity has evolved of federal programs establishing Underclass rights, protections, and entitlements; in effect, an identity endorsed by federal initiatives fundamentally referrant to and totally dependent upon the very existence of that benighted sector of society. It is unclear at what point the line was crossed when Underclass dependence on the Federal government transformed into governmental reliance on the existence of the Underclass; probably at or near the point when thinking about "poverty" came to be regarded as less a state out of which to work and more a state in which to generate, extend, and exploit entitlements. How could this come about? The sobering answer is likely that with all citizens playing by the same rules, "The Poor" conclusively showed that, by themselves, they could not work their way out of being poor, thus lending their plight to the enterprise of opportunistic political parties and "community" organizers. Thus, membership in the Underclass is now no longer a plight likely to encourage ambition to lift oneself to a higher socio-economic status but rather more a setting in which opportunity abounds for various subsidies, entitlements, support programs, free food, extensive child care programs, and even forgiveness of taxes all others have to pay to cover the expense of such benefits. And work does not seem to figure in the equation, making advancement into the independent, tax-paying, workaday world more a threat than an accomplishment. At the present time, a member's prospects would seem more promising through exploitation of mandated entitlements available below the so-called poverty line than by laboring at economic independence among the mainstream.

How can this come about, that the "Poor" become privileged beyond what is mandated and recognized of the working, contributing, sustaining, and tax-paying citizens? At least two factors seem to be at play. One is that the plight of the "Poor" has been taken humanely and compassionately to heart by our more successful citizens and has been granted the care and protection typically awarded an endangered species, much as was dying James Wait on the *Narcissus*. The other factor is that expressly for such tellingly

177

existential moments in a society's destiny, there are such things as politicians, votes, and the helpful guidance each is willing to offer.

17 September 2011

XXIV

The Untouchable

Given the great concern the people have for the changes which have been enacted by President Obama in the form as well as in the content of our government, such changes coupled as they are with an evolving re-working of the essential relationship of the American citizen to his government, it is no wonder that current political disquisition traces a fierce critique of the separate agendas come of party loyalties dividing the populace. Our essential two-party system gives ample room for the playing out of the citizen-government dyad in all its historical, philosophical, and societal particulars; and the inevitable points of contention, previously less urgently framed, now collect themselves into foci positing hard partisan policy generating those agendas. The two major nodal points of the discussion are the more comprehensive positions known separately as Conservative and Liberal, portrayed as they are in the American scene generally as Republican and Democrat. True, not all Conservatives are far Right, much less Free Market Republicans, and not all Liberals are far left, much less Socialism Democrats, but the trend is there though each party tends to gather its membership around a relatively centrist stance more palatable to the kinder and neighborly sensitivities of the people. Also, just as in war, prosecuted hostility is usually delegated to those specifically dedicated to its employment with commendable effort often made to limit collateral damage as much as possible. After all, even with martial hostilities, once the election is over we still have to live together as cooperatively as we can.

But the point is collateral damage and its inevitability. Politics often subsumes such misadventure under the euphemistic and blandishing collective known as "unintended consequences."

Truly, such damage was not ever really the purpose of the campaign, don't we know. But, the grim truth of it is that in hailing the conquering hero a certain majesty must be served, and bidden obeisance demands that unsightly damage come of his arrival be kept from view. But how does one keep such damage from view?

Verily it is not kept from view, and simply because we're obliged daily to live it out. More, it is a matter of how we restrict our notice of it. Various devices come to our rescue, some voluntary, some less so. One is the simple primitive, universal mechanism called Denial: we unconsciously refuse to recognize the existence of a problem as we busily go along with living it out. But Denial tends to be costly in that reality remains persistently and unabashedly intrusive with the result that arrears, known as unwelcome and distressing insights, come due from time to time and pop up demanding heavy expenditure of effort and energy in redoubled censorship. Such distressing insights, however, are almost never recognized initially as such, but more likely reckoned as our old friends, "unintended consequences," or their like. And certain things follow therefrom.

At this point we might appeal to Freud's *Future of an Illusion* for help in discerning our better way. This monograph cites the origin of religion as rooted in primitive man's psychical bent to see his surrounding reality in his own image, spirits and all, along with his need to defend himself against the cruelty and ravages of an impersonal and unpredictable environment. Means of appeasing the spirits, ultimately *The Spirit*, evolved over eons of evolutionary time, and as the spirits were to be appeased in accordance with canon law, so also were man's savage instincts sublimated into the rules and regulations basic to the civilizing process. The reader is referred to Freud's monograph for particulars, but suffice it to say that the more primitive the society and its reliance on religion for transitioning its development from the savage state to the establishment of civilization, the more the tribe's, or the society's, leader is held to be representative of The Guiding Spirit and necessarily its envoy. One need only note the great religions of the world to discern the general validity of this notion. One may also note that those same religions, played out across societies of differing levels of cultural development, display the various stages which those societies traverse on their way to the more sophisticated, scientific stage of the developmental sequence. Also, not all groups claiming the same faith are equally civilized, and a residual, contrapuntal savagery is often too visible in a worship style which keeps primitive illusions and barbaric practices quite close at hand. One need only be reminded of recent events in the Middle East and sub-Sahara Africa for examples of religious and tribal fervor engendering and endorsing extreme assaults upon civilized community.

What does this have to do with President Obama? Quite a lot when one considers the nature of his Presidency and the reaction of the population to it, and particularly so the rôle and performance of our legislators, writ large, as we would expect, in their response to his rôle as it arches far above and beyond the denotative meaning of his office. We know how the Constitution defines the rôle and purpose of his office—the *denotative* meaning of the Presidency—but rather it is the *connotative* meaning of Barack Obama's Presidency and his style of embracing it which is at point here.

It should not be lost on anyone that President Obama receives a remarkable degree of deference. True, a certain obeisance is rightly due in view of the office itself; it's the uniform, not the man who wears it no matter how improperly he does so, the military maxim goes. But even beyond that, he is granted a most gracious measure of leeway in his doings, executive and otherwise. True, the Office of President has more recently been pedestrianized, and also, by certain holders, even profaned, thus establishing its association with behaviors never before acceptable. True, the standard media, because of consanguinity of ideology, has been inordinately glowing in support of President Obama's performance despite all manner of his manifest shortcomings; their endorsement is both doctrinally obligated as well as politically prescribed. Also true is the circumstance that the opposition party, poised as it could be to exploit President Obama's rich trove of vulnerabilities come of past as well as present pursuits and associations, chooses to be characteristically bland in its obedient rôle as loyal and well-mannered opposition. But even the general populace, according to census, regard him favorably though most are quite opposed to his serving a second term. How can this be? Certainly any member of the opposition party, taking the nation to such straits as its people now fearfully endure, would be excoriated daily, loudly, and thoroughly by all, even likely by many of his own loyal following, were he to preside as does President Obama and yield the same general results. How so the difference?

Several reasons are offered, some plausible, some blandishing, and perhaps all a bit spurious. Foremost is the notion that since President Obama is the first Black man to inhabit the White House—an historical achievement in view of the fact that Black leaders elsewhere in the world hold much lesser standing in the international line-up whereas President Obama is the chief executive of the world's leading, richest power and one which earlier had *also* been slave-holding—and thus deserves most special accommodation. This reason rings of an Affirmative Action stance and may indeed apply to some degree in view of its widespread practice in this nation. But we see its relevance here as subsidiary at best.

Then there is the concern based on bias. The term "racist" has achieved the rank of sacrilege in this nation, at least in the public sector of personal damnation reckoning. Only in limited pockets of entrenched, avowed racism does it lack the cursedness of anathema to its bearers, and certainly almost all Americans fear being labeled racist in view of the social alienation and shame as would come to one charged so. Public figures, and especially politicians, know this exceedingly well and are keen to avoid any behavior an opponent or competitor could cite of them as deriving of racial prejudice, particularly prejudice against Blacks; anyone so accused would likely risk loss of credibility even if, and perhaps especially, his prejudicially suspect behavior prove justified, honest, and fair. As goes general commentary, criticism of Blacks, even if deserved, has risen to the level of *taboo* and, as with taboo, even if the offending criticism is based on reason, truth, and patent reality, it is still wrong on the basis of a higher, unchallenged proscription: it simply should not be done. Thus criticism of President Obama—a Black Commander-in-Chief and the very first one of his kind—would be blasphemous in the extreme if it in any way approached that as would be visited upon a White Commander-in-Chief performing similarly. President Obama simply is to be spared such for reasons which, yes, do include a special accommodation due his color. This special accommodation has led to the merry comment that he is to be Teflon-coated.

But even so, we do not believe taboo is enough to account for the restraint observed publicly by so many in any chanced criticism of President Obama. Our politicians will hurriedly suggest that electoral reasons be included. It is well known that approximately 95% of Black votes cast in the last Presidential election were cast for then Senator Obama. With Blacks numbering 12% of the nation's population, plus an even higher percentage of Hispanics of generally kindred leaning, the resulting block of votes can be, and is, decidedly determinative. Plus, if any members of this voter block subscribe to the sentiments and preferments mentioned thus far there seems to be at least reason enough to explain why fellow politicians in particular are loathe to criticize President Obama's performance, even if it is outrageous. Questions of political courage and integrity are thus called forth, but the legislative arena enjoys richest nourishment from a standing subsidy of opportunism, and a too keen criticism of President Obama's performance could well, and does, goad a rampant and vengeful sanctimony in the President's devoted and reliably protective media. Hence Republican timidity. As large a contribution as this may make to an embargo even on President Obama's deserved criticism, we see it as only additive, not essential, though nearly sufficient; a large part of the content, yes, but less an element of the form.

But some might urge keener note of the protective rôle of the standard media. No one can dispute that the standard media adores President Obama and sees his advent to the American political scene as Liberal Kingdom Come. The media's long-established left-leaning ideology has now emerged with the vigor and conviction of apotheosis in its support of President Obama and his policies. Indeed, the standard media is playfully regarded as Obama's public relations and propaganda arm. What is not so playful is the extent to which the media is willing to go to extol his actions, and worse, how silent it has been in the face of his malevolence toward the values and principles which have been the strength and majesty of this nation. The standard media's open and proactive alliance with his ideology is thus seen as an abiding discouragement of criticism as might rightfully come his way and so indeed likely contributes forcefully to suppression of open dissent, an effect perhaps suffered more especially by the simple and credulous. After all, if it cannot be told in Gath or published in Askelon where and how might it be known? As steady and pervasive as this suppressive power may be, we still do not account it as primary in protecting President Obama from the criticism as could rightfully come his way. The reluctance to criticize him, undoubtedly reinforced by the standard media's loyal advocacy, was already present well in advance of the media's accommodation and merely awaiting endorsement, or so it appears.

Inevitably the question of White guilt arises in any discussion of this kind. The dynamic presumed here would likely be driven by the Non-White citizenry. Such guilt, of itself, would seem to compel grant of a compensatory accommodation in any judgment of President Obama's efforts, representative as he is of his kind. It's a notion which generally goes unchallenged, and a sense of moral reckoning seasons the enlarged allowance brought to bear. In this moral reckoning there is to be noted also a handsome measure of genuine White good will in anticipation of his doing well at the task of office. This was clearly demonstrated by his sound electoral victory when so very little was known about him, even to include his

184

place of birth. Indeed, a very large and generous benefit of the doubt hopefully tendered.

So White guilt there is, undoubtedly. But just what is the nature of such guilt? The conventional answer is Slavery, and there is enough from that quarter to gratify any passing curiosity. But let's tarry for a moment to consider what else it might be which keeps the spectre of historical Slavery before us still. Certainly it is the very presence of the Black population itself, visibly bearing as it yet does the stigmata of having been enslaved in this land until five generations ago. But how does it happen that a condition which ended five generations ago endures in the ethos of our Black sub-culture such that its effect is before us daily? Moreover, an effect which sustains the Black sub-culture substantially at the relatively same socio-economic level as in the days of slavery, though now much more comfortably accommodated *pro rata* with the general material benefit come of inclusion in the collective American commonweal. While assuredly an improved status over that seen in the tribes of their origins in sub-Sahara Africa, just as the Whites and Orientals enjoy an improved status over their forebears in Europe and the Orient, the relative position of the Blacks, however, remains essentially the same, while that of the Orientals has moved up to parity with the Whites. Hence, Blacks still occupy the bottom position, globally or locally, history of institutionalized slavery or not. Thus, a broader perspective might view the Black culture's ethos and status in this country, so similar as it is in form to that of current African practice, as not so much burdened by historical slavery but moreso by limited cultural capacity, as stated in earlier offerings. Correspondingly, White guilt may draw more of its meaning from the inevitable and natural imbalance that comes of some participants' being evolutionary winners, and some losers. And President Obama, whatever may be his titular and institutional rôle, cannot help but bear spiritual identity with the Black Culture and its existential laments. And decency certainly forbids kicking, or criticizing, a man when he is down. This may help to explain polls which show that a significant majority of citizens oppose his having a second term, though a similar majority like him as a person.

These points should, in large part, address the question as to why President Obama is generally spared the criticism which assuredly would come of his political vulnerabilities were he White.

But we believe there is yet even more to say on the matter. All of the above points certainly bear on the issue, and some are seminal to what needs to be added, particularly those points raised in reference to the relative primitiveness of the Black culture, domestic as well as foreign. It has been pointed out that Black culture, still bearing large traces of an animistic orientation, is developmentally now reaching out to a more religious mode of thought. Thus, many of its leaders are anointed "Reverend." Moreover, at this very point in their history and in what they must see as their moment come for a giant leap forward, Black people now at last have a personal leader they not only can call "President," but also "our President" and have his meaning to them be as spiritual as it is political, and his mission as much deliverance as it is executive. In a word, the Black people finally have a Prophet all their own. It is thus safe to say that the Black people, especially the domestic ones, see President Obama's arrival as more than merely an electoral event. It is also meet to say that their devotion to him—why only 95% of the Black vote and not 100% is a phenomenon in itself—is more than just partisan turn out. Beyond being their leader he is their Savior, and his demeanor suggests that he is in full accord with the appellation. A long oppressed, deprived, and disparaged people, as they have seen themselves and generally with good cause, now see this time in their history as deliverance come. And President Obama clearly wishes it so as well. Hence his demeanor which, in no small part, bespeaks the mission of a Holy Man. *Their* Holy man, and to be seen so by all others.

Thus the line between religion and politics is blurred, not at all an uncommon feature in even advanced cultures which find need to sustain a protective insularity, but to the Black culture, only newly arrived at a religious mode of thought and in search of a Prophet, it

186

is a vitally important point of passage. In this regard the flag must follow the scepter. The Black Culture, long more aligned with tribal government than ever with national government, would see the scepter as transcending mere Constitutional authority, as certainly does President Obama himself. A consequent policy of this mode of thought is that Constitutional law is to be subordinated to capitular zeal, whatever its ideologic stripe, as long as it speaks of deliverance to the least advantaged of the human predicament; namely, the Black race, and, oddly, specifically to American Blacks. President Obama's unique national embassy results in such scenes as members of a Black para-military activist group showing up with truncheons in hand at a polling site to intimidate the voters in flagrant violation of Federal voting laws, and, though captured on video, escaping prosecution by the express order of the Department of Justice Attorney General, himself Black. Or the same Attorney General and his department engineering the illegal purchase of hundreds of assault weapons and smuggling them across the Mexican border to be made available to drug cartels for use in their criminal activities so that such may be cited as justification for increased gun control in this country, those very weapons used directly in criminal activities resulting in the death of hundreds of Mexican nationals and also one American Border Guard. And both cases tacitly sanctioned, if not specifically directed, by the White House. These cases are strong indicators of the lengths to which this Administration will go to achieve its political ends. When the nation's Attorney General sponsors, directs, and protects threatening and violent criminal activity one has to take a harder look at just what this Administration has in mind for the people of this nation.

Of course the loyal and partisan standard media and just about all Leftist groups have discounted the ominous import of these particulars, but as well the American people in general have given little account to such gross corruption and criminality. Congressional hearings have been mounted in pursuit of accountability in such criminality, but those hearings have been conducted with excru-

187

ciating restraint and decorum, and the tidy results thus far have amounted to little more than a cultivated scolding. The Attorney General has been defiant and contemptuous, safe in the sanction of Executive Privilege, and the President is majestically silent on the entire matter. And there seems to be no outrage anywhere, certainly none from the President's mainstay political party, and hardly any from the opposition party charged with the duty of monitoring the activities of incumbent opponents in protection of the American Commonwealth. Rather, there is the collective sense that President Obama is to be protected from accountability in these particulars as search is mounted for acceptable scapegoats, if any. This is not new in the register of Presidential Privilege and there are resounding examples of corruption of Justice in the catalogue of Presidential wrongdoing, even to the point of an impeached President being spared trial for high crimes and misdemeanors which included lying to a Grand Jury, but this is the first time, with perhaps the exception of those times of all-out international armed conflict, when the President is seen as being securely above the law. And above the flag as well.

But why in the case of President Obama? The conventional, seemly reasons have been given, but they all suffer from the taint of blandishment and lack the audible click of good fit. The cardinal reason would have to be one which subsumes the conventional ones as being only derivative, immediate or remote. It would have to be universal, not at all transient, and certainly not readily amenable to open address. It would also have to be odiously unacceptable to conventional and preferred thinking for it to have avoided open notice thus far. And, assuredly, it would have to be proof to any effort at remediation as could be countenanced by the collective gender.

By the stark process of elimination, such reckoning directs us to an element of our environment which may not intrude too often upon our awareness, perhaps so by design, much as with the fish which, among all the elements of his environment, is least likely to

188

be aware of the water in which he swims. So with us, that something so pervasive in our world of daily living that we mark it little except when there's disturbance, threat, or "change."

As we've said, we strongly and unequivocally believe that we're all looking the other way to avoid the shock of seeing full clear President Obama's burning hatred of White America. Everybody prefers to avoid dealing with another's hatred, especially so if directed one's way for being the hated one, or thing, or some part of it. Moreover, his hatred anoints him the ordained leader of a long restive, sometimes violent Black America in its unremitting stress of trying to fit itself successfully to a scientific–technical society when its own Culture Capital is so limited. In this regard President Obama is the man of "his people," as the Attorney General has said. Plus, as stated above, Black America, in its early stage of the religious mode of conceptual thinking, is compelled to see President Obama as a Savior come, a Holy Man, the Prophet, just as he must see himself in accordance with his Muslim beliefs. It is a perfect fit of an oppressed people finally receiving a Prophet, one specifically their own, for a destined salvation and the glory of freedom; freedom once again and now total.

Now, who in good conscience, hearing such background music, and we're sure most of us do, even non-believers, criticize such a person as one might some ordinary, dissembling, opportunistic politician? Few among us, for sure. Most people are much too mindful of the double jeopardy come of being heavy-handed in detailing the checkered pedigree of a charismatic leader who is both Black *and* his people's Prophet. No politics there; only blasphemy. And certainly no place for the squeamish, as Islam has hideously demonstrated in its own take on such matters, matters assuredly brought to President Obama's attention in his early religious training.

We are all mindful of how volatile Black groups can be. There is no shortage of remembered riots erupting over seemingly local and limited events, stoking, because of their larger reference, a spreading conflagration of violence, much as a spark applied to

189

waiting tinder. These riots, such as in Los Angeles and Detroit, overwhelmed the law enforcement agencies and had to burn themselves out along with that part of the municipality set to flame. Murder, rape, plundering occurred in concert with a raging ferocity, which has to be seen as tribal in its primitiveness, much as is still the case in sub-Sahara Africa, the thin veneer of civilization too readily shed in the tribal passions of some evocative moment. Most people of this nation, especially the White population, do not wish to think that such violence may lurk below the surface of the workable interracial amity we generally have, and this preference is supported by a de facto separation of the races in that they tend to live in separate realms. But the indications are there: it is estimated that eighty-five percent of violent crimes in this nation are committed by Blacks, and, correspondingly, that eighty-five percent of the prison population is Black. Nor can it be ignored that in at least one large northeastern city there is a standing threat that if a certain Black leader is executed, duly tried and sentenced though he be for murdering a police officer, "this town will burn if he burns." These points are offered as indicators of a certain flammability of the Black race which, in this nation, such as the deep South where the Black population may outnumber the White, has long supported a grim concern.

It is suggested that to varying degrees this concern is upon all of us, Black and White alike, and that a large part of that concern is based on a fear that once such violence erupts it will, if in response to a widespread national issue embracing all of us, spread rapidly and concertedly. It is also suggested that such is significantly more likely to occur if pre-election campaigning too aggressively addresses President Obama's gross vulnerabilities come of his attacking private enterprise, weakening our military posture, diminishing our international standing, curtailing our personal liberties, and attempting to undermine the Constitution, not to mention his damning and nether associations earlier, and currently, in his political career. While his White opponent will be treated to a full menu of negative cam-

190

paigning, turnabout will assuredly be regarded taboo, perhaps even blasphemy by his most ardent, sectarian followers, and the nation already has enough to do in defending against violence mounted by religious fanatics of another frontier, but curiously kindred in complaint. It is this confection of hatred, bitterness, vengefulness, and a volatility come of a group's limited impulse control which forms a hovering dread urging gentle accommodation of President Obama on the campaign trail. Otherwise, aggravated anger might erupt into open violence. Plus, there is the mutual dread that a resounding defeat of President Obama might be seen as the last vanishing hope of a benighted people in their desperate reach for comity and equality. And, in view of President Obama's perfervid sense of mission and ordained purpose, there is chill concern that in the face of falling pre-election poll numbers there might come an "October Surprise" in the form of escalated foreign hostilities as would rally the electorate to patriotic unity in the face of national threat.

All of this, and likely much more unknown to us, forms the reason President Obama has thus far been spared the rough and tumble of political campaigning usually experienced by others. His vivid vulnerabilities and the attendant possible consequences come of addressing them in the raw imposes a definite restraint on free-wheeling electioneering as would otherwise come his way. The result is that there are two standards, one suitable to him, the other to his opponent, with the advantage of ranging maneuver going to him and his party simply because the opposition party is not especially given to slash and burn in the face of defeat. Quite the contrary; indeed, the opposition party is rather much too given to polite and dutiful accommodation in its standard rôle as loyal opposition. But the people themselves, eschewing the wretched plight of holding a tiger by the tail, may come to speak above and beyond such kindly efforts at détente and proceed to mandate their own form of "change" which just might in no way accommodate President Obama's grand agenda. And we shall see.   01 December 2011

XXV

Arma Virumque Cano

So what is left?

Our discussion has visited some of the salient points highlighting features of our present lot as a nation confronting the evolution of our Democracy and its vicissitudes. We have tarried more on some points than on others in the belief that the points singled out had more to offer in speaking the meaning of the moment. The result has been a discussion swept along by the currents of daily happenstance we experience as the American way of Life. The swell of such are read as distinctive and revealing trends of our time, speaking as much to their own moment as to the nature of their origins. In this regard President Obama, about whom much has been said in these offerings, is featured as a symptom of our *general* and *national* discontent though writ large in keeping with his own *personal* mission. The citizenry, primarily those of the common gender, are seen as the expression of the larger message along with some estimate of the measure of their appreciation of its meaning. The larger message is that the nation is in serious decline though the populace, through its political leaders, seems unable to do anything about it except, in keeping with the purest of Greek irony, to hasten the process along by the very measures undertaken to forestall its inevitability. Indeed, agencies and institutions are noted to be well along in their drift to *reductio ad absurdum* in that they are progressively transmuting into their own antitheses. A case in point is our government itself.

For example, it is a given that the prime rôle of the President of the United States is to protect the Constitution. His job description, plus his vow of office, are built upon that basic duty. But, as said, it is clear that President Obama does not like this nation, and

193

likes its Constitution even less. He, his Cabinet and his closest followers have been tireless in their efforts to undermine the Constitution and the Nation's founding principles in favor of an ideology the people would never approve in open vote. Thus his administration has been shot through with dissemblance, deceit, and frank lawlessness. And his party members serve as enablers, either by commission or omission. Thus there is an aura of crisis in the air, and all among us sense a national danger come (see Entry XXIV).

But not only in government do we see such corruption and degeneracy but in the business world as well. Prudent, continent, law-abiding enterprise seems not to apply anymore. It appears that the rules of decency, honesty, and fair play no longer have a place. The banking industry in concert with kindred government excess, has demonstrated reckless avarice on a scale previously unimaginable with the result that the taxpayer is left the galling onus of funding and sustaining a Government-Banking collusion rooted in usury and venality. It is clear that both Congress and the Banking Industry, by virtue of President Obama's default as protector of the Constitution, greet the national treasury as booty ripe for ravishment by power voluptuaries only too keen to exploit the generous hospitality of an innocent, credulous populace. President Obama is to be counted as foremost of the voluptuaries, the Lord of Calculated Misrule, in the best tradition of cynical legislative abandon while an awakening electorate longs for the restoration of Columbia's majesty as well as its moral as well as fiscal solvency. The political scene has now become one in which need to reverse the national regression of the past several years has become paramount though the White House, and much of Congress, see in the exploitation of electoral simplicity a singular opportunity to aggrandize their agendas for subverting and erasing the normal and natural consequence of individual differences by standardizing human endeavor to the lowest common denominator. Personal ambition, talent, and enterprise are thus to be seen as selfish and immoral. But, the electorate might, and hopefully will, ask who would want to live in a nation so blunted? Clearly, those who have little to lose and something to gain. In a word, those who have so very little to give but who covet so very much. The restoration of Columbia requires that such persons remain in the minority. President Obama, who hates and is determined to destroy Columbia, is actively recruiting such needy types to enlarge the ranks of those willing to adopt officially-defined personal values in the formation of an alliance with others of lesser capacity in the establishment of an electoral majority willing to forfeit a free, individualized, open future for a closed, defined, regulated societal rôle, much as one sees with tribes, as we've said earlier. History speaks loudly on such points.

But History isn't taught anymore. The national Education thrust currently focuses on the social issues of the day and thus bears directly on the political orientation defining those issues and the particulars such orientation cites as points of seminal importance. Thus Education is now less a free-ranging exploration of man's treasury of knowledge and more a focused approach to a preferred sociologic highlighting of political currents in the daily experience, partisan accents included. Hence, Education in this nation has taken on the quality of a social orientation, even indoctrination, with some quite partisan policies clearly preferred over fact, with Heritage, History, and Constituted Principle subordinated to the fitful winds of political expediency. One grim consequence of this trend is that the teaching profession has adopted a credo which focuses on immediate content at the expense of enduring form—the drama of today's news story is more instructive than the distilled teachings of History, so it is felt. Correspondingly, the teaching profession has of late oriented itself more to personal benefit than to professional ethic, and the everyday, dedicated teacher now has the task of reconciling the two. The profession has become politicized, unionized, and victimized by aggressive partisan groups (see Entry XI) eager to broaden a voter base at the expense of individual freedom and integrity. And, as has been openly admitted, even at the expense of the children.

Now, then, what's to be said about our political leaders? So much already has been said in earlier offerings it's not easy to know what else could be added without inviting tedium. Perhaps merely a bit of emphasis might suffice. Such emphasis just might parallel the boost public entitlement lends to the advent of egregious political types. To wit, an alert and searching electorate tends to exercise a restraining effect on the rise of aberrant and anomalous political entities, though they be at all times quietly and patiently awaiting their moment. But should the electorate drift into a palmy complacency suited to a mounting sense of entitlement which bequeaths ranging civic initiative to its legislators, such personages will surface, usually in the keep of some equally peculiar ideology to give them thrust and moment while the electorate dozes, as very much seems to be the design with President Obama and his following. In the offing and in that regard, a trove of opportunism looms, spawned of envy and vengefulness, neither of which would have much traction with an alert and discerning populace committed more to national well-being than to personal disport. But politicians, too often reflecting the worst of their constituency, will of course take their electoral sustenance as it comes, national health be damned. Thus, we now see a downward drift from nationhood to class struggle. In a word, back to tribes and their parochial enmities, President Obama's special predilection as well as his existential bent. Undoubtedly, this regressive tendency is present in all of us, though it is usually subordinated to cultural growth and national achievement. Nevertheless, back to the tribe and, here again and especially so, the nation be damned.

At this point we might ask if there is any institution out there which still embraces and indeed practices integrity, honesty and dignity? The profession of Medicine has been recruited into the armamentarium of class warfare strategy and, with Federal participation in licensing, utilization, and remuneration, the individual practitioner is pressed into the ranks of the suborned, and with a lamentable lack of kicking and screaming as one would certainly expect of the profession's National Medical Societies. The States' Medical Societies tend to be more outspoken on the matter.

The Church itself has been proselytized, and, having always had close kinship to Sociology in its enlarged conception of Theology, now sees its ministry encouraged by partisan design to address politically the classes of American society as well as the internecine conflicts deriving of those classes, to include the Nation's moral failing in the impoverishment of victims both domestically and abroad. Moral condemnation of America is generally implicit, often resoundingly explicit, in President Obama's pronouncements which never lack accent on just deserts finally at hand and typically to take the form of overdue, righteous, political preferment and economic compensation due those abused. His mission and manner carry the mark of the Seer, and his tone is that of a reckoning long in coming, his message taking its stamp from his identification with his mentor's ministry. Plus, the focus on spiritual failings of this Nation tends to keep at a convenient distance unsettled and crampy questions as to his own personal creed. And the American church is remarkably compliant with, even resonant to, the tune of it all, but at the cost of a regrettable doctrinal susceptibility.

Moving on, we now direct the lens of scrutiny to our Judiciary. Here we see the infiltration of one division of government by another in search of a way to circumvent the legislative process. The result is an embattled Judiciary internally conflicted and contested between those who would wish to use it as a pathway for legislation rejected by the standing legislative process, and those who would have this constituted division of the government keep to the purpose of interpreting the Constitution and its lawful reach in cases of dispute as may come forth. Hence, the contenders consist of those who hold the Constitution to be the fundamental guide to the juridical integrity and legality of the daily business of America, and those who regard it as a dated document which needs to be adjusted to suit the times; specifically, that the Judiciary be modified to serve as sanctuary for selected failed legislation and function as a competitor

197

with the Congress in the legislative process. Legislators from the bench, the merry phrase runs. Thus the appointment process in Federal judgeships assumes vast importance in that it now features partisanship so much more than it favors juridical skill and learning. Our courts, especially on the Federal level, are thus corrupted by agendas not ennobled by the ideals of jurisprudence. And, once again, our legislators are merely Present.

But the practice is aggravated beyond toleration by the gross malfeasance of a lawless Attorney General Office whose activities are openly designed to undermine the nation's Constitution. Felonious means are used to enlist the assistance of foreign criminals in mounting assaults upon key elements of the Constitution in an effort to render the American populace more docilely acquiescent to *Government* control, this in treasonous violation of the fundamental precept that the government is of, for, and by the people and right-fully under *Citizen* control. Such an initiative is unquestionably a strategy issuing from the Oval Office which protects the perpetrators who, in kind, protect President Obama so that the most grievous con-demnation as might come his way for his rôle in this crime is that he also is merely Present but sanctimoniously aware of his paternal duty to soothe and reassure a distressed citizenry and also any of the less compliant of his following. Thus, in a broader sense, criminality and treason are institutionalized, and this bespeaks a political agenda come of an ideology antithetical to that of America as History, the World, and Americans know it. And President Obama presides over this attempted and so far bloodless domestic coup d'etat, except for the life of one American Border Patrol guard and that of untold hundreds of Mexican Nationals, all of whom were programmed as expendable, their deaths perhaps seen as operationally necessary in the successful prosecution of the coup. And, once again, except for a vigilant and outraged few, our legislators, and especially the ones more favorably partisan to the President, are recorded as merely Present. In the overall, we are reminded of Washington's "grazing multitude."

Our opening question was whether the national degeneracy spearheaded by the current Administration has spared any institution of the corruption it cultivates as its means of corroding the national will. To wit, is there any institution left that embraces and practices Honor, Dignity, and Integrity in address of its proper duties, rather than the enervating, disingenuous, cynical posturing orchestrated by the White House in its management of the Beltway Commune? There seems to be, but its preservation also seems to depend on its operational distance from the flagpole—the farther away the better, just as appears to be the case with most endeavors of the American people. This thus far spared institution is the American Military. Despite all else experiencing decay in this nation our Military remains the finest in the world today, a position our other institutions used to hold. And, of course, having yet among us so fine and patriotic an element in our national mix is inimical with the Obama Agenda, especially so since the Attorney General's office so miserably bungled the opening tactic in its strategy to disarm the American populace, thus revealing the covert and creeping danger being unwittingly advanced by a popular complacency which sees threat to this nation as coming only from foreign sources alien to our way of life. The greater danger, it is now clear, comes from within, and, ironically, from those chambers founded and empowered ex- pressly for the purpose of preserving and protecting this nation's safety and exceptionalism. Tragically for all, those chambers are now being used by occupants, chosen as they were by an uninformed and credulous populace, as a salient from which to exploit a corrosive national complacency in fulfillment of the covert coup being mounted. But, in the event that an aroused citizenry refuses to be disarmed, it then becomes necessary to disable whatever *else* is in place to protect this nation's safety. If such happens to be a fine, patriotic, and dedicated Military thus far essentially untainted by the collective governmental corruption and degeneracy, then one should now expect concerted effort by the Administration to strip the Military of its sinews in reinforcement of *political* primacy for the prosecution of the Administration's agenda which, it has been proposed, is to punish White America and to reduce it to a featureless Welfare State where individual differences are proscribed and discounted. In effect, a Holy Mission to protect the World's most populous endangered species, the Black race.

But America may come to realize its own dire endangerment and resist the enfeeblement of its Military, seemingly the *only* remaining American institution which still embraces courage, integrity, and patriotic dedication. The general citizenry might well find need to turn to it to regain a strength and purpose it itself has lost. Leadership within the Military will then be crucial to the event and some contamination by the general National degeneracy may, and likely will, be revealed in the military command structure since it is an old Army maxim that all young soldiers are brave, dedicated, and fiercely loyal but many, upon reaching the rank of Colonel, become politicians, even in a wholesome environment so much less cynical and degenerate as does now seem to be before us. Fortunately, the common ranks outnumber those so politically drawn, and, most definitely in this case, there is safety in numbers which would include even the old soldiers now in mufti as plain citizens. Regrettably, the Administration's thus far relatively bloodless effort at coup d'etat may, because of fanatical sectarian elements in President Obama's following, escalate the conflict to the level of open violence in keeping with the known volatility of his kind. Such would seem unconscionable to the patriotic, law-abiding American citizens, but likely not to President Obama's lawless administration in the face of desperation. This grim and horrid prospect would perhaps finally alert the American populace to the wisdom of Sir Francis Bacon's warning that "Nothing doth more hurt in a state than that cunning men pass for wise."

15 February 2012

200

XXVI

The Question

In 2008 the American people, acting on blind faith and breathtaking naiveté, elected as President of the United States and Leader of the Free World a man of whom they knew virtually nothing other than the color of his skin. Running on a platform of "Hope and Change" Barack Obama, America's first Black president, was able to win the trust of the electorate, having been spared the intense scrutiny of the usually ruthless standard media in its vetting of any opposition presidential candidate. The time has now passed to ask who the actual Barack Obama is. The important question to ask now is who are we, the American people, to allow ourselves to be misled so far from our better selves by a man who has proclaimed as his mentor his pastor of twenty years who called upon God to "Damn America"; a man who as a community organizer-cum-agitator, taught minority groups how to play the Race card in extorting handouts from individuals and businesses; a man who, as an Illinois State Senator, opposed successive versions of a bill to protect babies born alive after failed abortions, certainly the ultimate suppression of a God-given individual right; a man who taught constitutional law, but was chagrined at the Constitution's restrictions on increased government control, completely missing its fundamental purpose even though as President of the United States he would nominally swear to "preserve, protect and defend" that very Constitution; a man whose wife declared upon his election that for the first time in her adult life she was proud to be an American, revealing a feeble knowledge about the birth of this nation as well as an abundance of self-absorption.

The people with whom Barack Obama has chosen to surround himself offer a very telling picture of the man and his antipathy to the ideals that make America exceptional. The very core of that exceptionalism is the belief that men are capable of governing themselves and that each individual is endowed by his Creator with unalienable rights. How can one believe that President Obama supports individual rights when he would deny life-saving care to babies who survived failed abortion attempts? How can one believe he supports the rights of the smallest minority, the individual, when he has spoken of his belief in "collective salvation," a phrase used by some Black pastors who believe the White race should relinquish its power and return the wealth it "stole from the Black man." It is clear from President Obama's policies that he is actively pursuing redistribution of wealth, demonizing the wealthy, and exhorting the successful to "pay their fair share."

The profound arrogance of Barack Obama in his apparent belief that he is capable of delivering cosmic social justice has gone largely unaddressed by our mainstream media. It speaks volumes that as the arbiter of social justice he would appoint as his Attorney General an individual so consumed with hatred for the White race that he allows to go unchallenged a group of Black thugs in pseudo-military garb to wield clubs and threaten voters at the polls in the city where our founding documents were created. Astonishingly, this same group of Black thugs later placed a million dollar "wanted dead or alive" bounty on the head of a White man involved in the death of a young Black man with not a single word from either the President or the Attorney General in denunciation of this outrageous affront to the rule of law. Their failure even to make an attempt at soothing rampant passions was likely interpreted by too many as license to perpetrate violence against Whites. Such incidents of violence against Whites have been suppressed by the media, as demonstrated by a newspaper in Virginia that failed to report the beating of two of its White reporters by a Black mob.

At this point we need to ask ourselves why we would vote for any man without knowing the content of his character or even asking him what his vision for America holds. We believe every person who voted for Barack Obama truly wanted him to succeed, but perhaps for very separate reasons. On the one side there likely were many who voted for him out of a spirit of generosity and good will, wanting to give a Black man a chance to excel at the highest office in the land. However, on the other side there were many who saw in him an opportunity to exact revenge and/or to procure copious entitlements from the wealthy whom the more credulous citizenry had been led to believe had acquired their wealth unfairly or dishonestly.

Both views could not be more un-American, the former group because of their misguided use of Affirmative Action in their selection of a President and thus guilty of a "soft racism" which identifies all members of certain groups as also-rans in life and incapable of succeeding on their own merit; the latter group for lack of the basic American ideals of self-reliance and self-determination and all too willing to trade their freedom for handouts.

President Obama is the ultimate proof that Affirmative Action, however well-intentioned, is doomed to failure because it demands the suspension of reality, divorcing honest assessment of performance from outcomes. The American people gave Barack Obama a unique opportunity only a few score men have ever had, and placed their faith in him to do his best for *all* Americans. Alas, President Obama squandered this opportunity by choosing to divide Americans against one another; black against white; rich against poor, elderly against the young; the federal government against the states; and even women against men so as to rob productive citizens of the fruits of their labors and to deprive the poor of their dignity by perpetuating a malignant dependency on government.

This leads back to the crucial question of what have *we*, the American people, become? Benjamin Franklin once wrote, "Only a virtuous people are capable of freedom. As nations become corrupt and vicious, they have more need of masters." Are we now no longer capable of governing ourselves and therefore in need of masters? Have we, in a creeping degeneracy, settled on electing the same

203

self-serving politicians again and again because they reflect our own base self-serving natures? Have too many of us become content to allow government to rule us as long as it continues to dole out to us the wealth of others? Have we become the grazing multitude with whom President Washington had issue, such that "cunning, ambitious, and unprincipled men will be enabled to subvert the power of the people and to usurp for themselves the reins of government, destroying afterwards the very engines which have lifted them to unjust dominion?" If so, we will forever bear the blame of being the selfish generation which allowed the grand American experiment of self-government to perish. We will have failed not only the great Hope of our Founding Fathers who were willing to pledge their lives, their fortunes, and their sacred honor for our freedom, but we will have failed our posterity and delivered them to bondage.

In November 2012 the American people will speak to that very question.

2 June 2012

XXVII

Vox Populi

The hurlyburly's done; the battle's lost and won. The people have spoken, and now to meet with the dénouement of the election and what we—SWC, myself, and undoubtedly many, many others—fear will be a calamitous assault upon the traditional freedoms known to our way of life, freedoms and rights which perhaps too many of the voting populace enjoy as a simple given and likely also regard as wholly unalienable. But not so by some important others who see those very freedoms and rights as negotiables which vexedly restrict the rôle of government and much too pointedly define the American way of life; to wit, the Individual and his Rights as standing primary and the government subordinate to the perpetuation of those rights and their effects. And we all—*all*—know that President Obama certainly does not see the rôle of government in the same light. Indeed, there is ample reason to believe he sees America, as it was intended and instituted, irreconcilably antagonistic to his own conception of government as the centralized engine and arbiter of a comprehensive communal existence which defines the individual's rôle and meaning, the individual's own conception of himself having little societal significance, much less meaning. It has been said earlier (see entries III, IV) that President Obama hopes to re-figure our governing bodies as they now stand, re-align our social structure, establish the means of sustaining such changes, and use whatever enactments and initiatives as may be necessary to guarantee the effectiveness of those changes. Individual differences, rather than being credited and honored, are to be subordinated and, ideally, minimized in their societal and industrial effect because, as is too well known, left to their own devices those differences will inevitably lead to a layering of social and economic class. Such a result is by all means to be

205

prevented, particularly if those class differences shake out too visibly along racial lines. And, as has been stated earlier, President Obama intends to save the Black race from technologic-industrial extinction, and, accordingly, protect thereby a certain electoral reliability for his following. Such appears to be his strategy, and his tactic is the missive of an archaic Communism which posits everybody equal by need, save those overseeing the system itself. Also, it has earlier been said, President Obama seems to have an enduring, well nigh impenetrable conception of himself as the one to achieve, Prophet-like, this national and social transformation.

So much for a brief review.

And now, what might we expect over the next several years? It all depends on the shape and scope, aided by a predominantly self-serving and obliging Congress, of President Obama's Vision, plus his determination to defend and implement that Vision. I say "Vision" with a touch of unrepentant charity since President Obama's design for this nation, and quite possibly all "infidel" others in suit, carries nothing of the inspiring, uplifting *élan* usually associated with that term. Not at all, and more on that later. But for our present purpose that word will do.

Now that President Obama has a second term and need not worry about re-election we think there will be, along with its disclosing indicators, a more vigorous playing out of his quite *personal* agenda. We will also see a bolder, franker display of his political *style* in effecting the changes he wishes. A case in point is the recent terrorist attack resulting in the tragic death of our Libyan ambassador and three of his defenders at the Consulate in Benghazi. The attack there ran counter to President Obama's celebrated re-election campaign plank proclaiming that he had decapitated Al Qaeda in having bin Laden killed, and, as a result, the Middle East was now on its way to becoming a more stable, more manageable arena for his having set Al Qaeda "back on its heels." But the terrorist attack put lie to that halcyon contention, and the Administration, from the top down, went into frantic and convoluted damage

206

control—not control of damage to our Consulate and its personnel, but control of damage to President Obama's reassuring rhetoric promising a more consanguine Arab Spring, one more congenial to his re-election campaign efforts. The Consulate, our Ambassador, and his three defenders, were thus declared expendable in disallowance of any rescue effort as would have amplified global attention to the folly and cynicism of President Obama's claim of having scotched Al Qaeda to advance the cause of Middle East peace in our times.

Such is the *manifest* content of that grisly episode. Though management of the episode and its sequelae qualifies as criminal in negligence, incompetence, and gross malfeasance, we believe it is just a joltingly palpable aspect of a deeper and vastly more ominous aberration assaulting the instituted rôle of the American Presidency and that of our Congress. Given that perhaps the terrorist attack happened upon more than it intended or expected; or that the Consulate was perhaps covertly serving as a base for gun-running— or something—to Syria—or somewhere—via Turkey; or that a larger contingent of the Consulate (rescued and held incognito as well as incommunicado even today) were the operatives in that pursuit, it seems that the larger strategy and more compelling tactic was to protect that shadow operation from open disclosure primarily because such would undoubtedly have magnified the hollow mockery of President Obama's staged rôle as Envoy of Peace and thus risk having his re-election hopes become a casualty as well. We're also sure that if and when this suspect aspect of the Benghazi incident is disclosed it will be previewed thoroughly by a procession of sanctimonious pronouncements that the civil war in Syria—or somewhere—had spawned such unspeakable atrocities that Humanity alone compelled our considered intervention. It is fully imaginable that some such blandishment could actually be offered to cover the cost of four American lives. It's so unfortunate that the Ambassador, who was left behind, and his three would-be rescuers are not alive today to help clarify this ugly enigma. No tale can now be told by them.

It is eminently clear that President Obama presents himself, Prophet–like, as ordained to deliver the people, particularly our Nation's Black contingent, to a Marxist Promised Land. To do so, he has undertaken the task of tearing down the temples of Free Enterprise and Personal Freedom and replace them with an enlarged, centralized government capable of generating a monolithic society in which regulated and apportioned need is the great leveler, not opportunity. This design has been identified in earlier entries, but what hasn't been emphasized is how this format, though historically registered as one of the several possible forms of government, offers us also a template of President Obama's own personal psychic structure, not the least part of which is his root identity. More to the point, it is possible to glimpse telling aspects of his mind and its nature by what we can now witness as the stress behavior of his administration and the defenses it employs to sustain some semblance of functional integrity in the face of evolving difficulty. Specifically, more tell-tale scandals are to come, and more symptoms will surely surface. Thus, we may get a fuller view of the form and content of President Obama's own thought processes by observing their externalizations in the cast of the goals, the methods, and the character of his administration. Hence, our government, as it now stands, is more an expression of *himself* and his singular sense of purpose than it is a tripartite function consisting of executive, judicial, and legislative branches as originally constituted. It is now centralized in the *executive* sector for defining national policy, purpose, method, and meaning—all in keeping with President Obama's conception of his own personal calling. The quintessential raison d'être of America—the Individual and his Liberty—is being replaced by the Prophet and his Vision. Moreover, the stripe of too many sitting Congressional politicians is egregiously enabling of such, either out of devotion, or fear, or mere profit. The government of, for, and by the *people* is now anecdotal. Call such a phenomenon

208

the making of a Prophet, or Messiah, or Dictator, or even a King. History offers abundant examples of each and also the Destiny each carries, but the larger madness of it all is that so many of this Nation's citizens idly stand by in witness, obligingly complying in the name of Hope, all the while forfeiting their rights, which tells us something of Mens Populi.

Thus we can now look upon his administration in its workings, its methods, and its apparent goals as a template tracing the Form and Content of President Obama's own psychic structure, along with its orientation, in his self-styled mission to deliver upon the Hope and Change he proclaimed, plus also conveying more frankly just exactly what he meant by such. Firstly, his administration has shown an amazing disregard for established law unless it can be applied to his own purposes. The effort to undermine the Second Amendment by the bungled "Fast and Furious" operation, initiated by the Oval Office (read President Barack Obama) and implemented by the Department of Justice is a case in point. Protecting that operation and its perpetrators by way of stealth, deceit, dissimulation, denial, and frank lying in the face of patent disclosure, coupled with indifference to, perhaps even the suggestion of contempt for, its tragic consequences, gives us a window on what earlier has been noted of President Obama's driving hatred of White America, its founding principles, and particularly its checks and balances method of governmental process. He and his Administration, the latter an extension of the former but essentially one and the same, notwith-standing the occasional disclaimers by the former in response to the tacky, wretched blunders of the latter, reveal on a broad scale the mind and method of the President in his assault upon the traditional American way of life. Specifically, our exceptionalism is to be re-placed by a general collectivism, and no citizen will be exempt of this great leveling except the Prophet himself and his apostolic following. Indeed, as much as this outrageous and impeachable example of governmental criminality commands public attention, especially the dogged efforts on the part of the perpetrators to deceive the public as to the scope, the authorship, and the purpose of that failed assault on the Second Amendment, what also to be seen is not only the frantic efforts to protect the President and his Administration, but also something much more generative of the mix, and also so much more morbid. I think those who are enlisted to his political goals, perhaps many only obliquely, are basically given more to the protection of the animus of his Vision which is, we believe, an organized and articulated mental construct generating his meaning to himself and thus his basic relationship to his experiential world. Specifically, we believe President Obama has a fixed belief that he is indeed a Prophet ordained to lead the Black race to salvation, a mission providentially to begin here in America where Black subjugation was institutionalized as part of governmental policy. Thus, in this calling, he is morally above the law of such a long-oppressive government as ours, as he sees it, just as is also his Administration, plus a significant sector of his followers, which, the election has shown, numbers in the millions, and he likely also believes that he answers to no one but some cosmic imperative, such as an astral Father, guiding him in cleansing this nation's Temples of its enslavers, money changers, oppressors, and usurpers along with their self-serving White racist documents they use as testament. Hence, his apology tours around the world.

And, much like some other Prophets of old, he came out of nowhere. And, as is usual with such Prophets, those who oppose him are de facto enemies of the Word and are to be vanquished out of hand by any means necessary since they are unworthy of the Coming, even if their eradication means the sacrifice of innocents. Not at all unlike what we've come to know of Islamic extremism.

In that regard Benghazi is certainly a case in point. Consulate personnel were sacrificed in keeping with the need to sustain the President's image of Grand Deliverance for the many, albeit through the required sacrifice of some; and this assize, arrived at by him and implemented accordingly, was suppressed from public view as necessary to protect his mission, his Vision, and his re-election

210

hopes. To the forgivably naïve, it was merely his re-election being protected, but on the level of his meaning and destiny it was his essential and transcendent Calling sore at risk. His immediate following likely knew this and thus *served as called*, doing so against the backdrop of Benghazi's Danteish scene so very far removed from the Law and Order of a Representative Democracy. And, not at all oddly, his followers still serve, and do so in keeping with the ruthless practices of that savage region. Moreover, protection of President Obama's Savior image and its imperatives demands that his whereabouts during the time of the Benghazi attack remain enigmatic. Protocol in such matters holds it quite infra dig that Prophets be seen in brawling conflict with opposing forces; they best remain removed and above such coarse strife which more suitably is managed by apostles and devoted following. Prophets look best in an unsullied beatitude. But the reality may be that he and his inner sanctum were feverishly at work setting the scene for the sacrifice of our Ambassador while developing a diversionary story to hide the covert activities of the Consulate, and hence the President's preferred image. But then again he might have been temporarily removed from it all enjoying a relaxing moment of lotus. Thus, on the manifest level, the tragedy is conveniently to be regarded as a regrettable spontaneous incident out of step with the salutary and wholesome sweep of his ministry aimed at the greater good of that troubled region, and definitely not to be seen as a runaway, wretched terrorist negation of promised Deliverance. Forswear such, since if seen on that more basic, latent level the incident could threaten to topple the consensually validated idealized construction of himself as the Prophet of this time, ordained to deliver salvation in his own image. We say "consensual" because, after all, didn't the American people, or at least enough of them, believe so of him and elevate him to the position he now holds and from which he will take them to full communal equality long denied them by certain tyrannous founding documents? And as for that most noisome distraction in Benghazi, various disciples and loyal retainers can assure us all that it was merely an aberration caused by the gross and offensive indiscretions of a churlish infidel so alien to the cause, actually irrelevant but regrettably problematic to the President's ministry.

Thus, because we believe that President Obama's personal agenda derives from more than mere political ambition and thereby transcends the ordinary restraints and corrective effect a sterner reality of checks and balances would and should impose, we expect that much more will evolve of his dysgenic effect upon our various government agencies. Cunning and stealthy insinuation into standing government agencies for the purpose of subverting their legitimate function and suborning them into alignment with his larger design will likely become the background music of his usual pabulum rhetoric as his followers, many of whom now work in the civic sector, stand all too ready to do his bidding. We feel parlous times are ahead and resistance by the more concerned element of our society will likely goad him into bolder and more extreme attempts to fulfill his calling. We believe he will never be able to credit what may very soon become the re-considered wishes of the majority of this nation's citizens because, after all, so very many of them are so unforgivably guilty in any event; at least in *his* mind.

But for it all, and in view of the speculations we offer above, there is little doubt in *our* mind as to who gave the "stand down" order to stay our rescue forces poised to rush to the Consulate's defense. A few courageous Americans, outraged at the sacrifice intended, rightly violated that vile order and gave their utmost to protect what was ours. We are yet to hear the Administration's view on the nobility of *their* selfless effort, defying as it did both the Administration's "stand down" order as well as Jihadist barbarity.

18 February 2013

XXVIII

Mene, Mene Tekel Upharsin

Many of us are familiar with Belshazzar's Feast which he held to celebrate the glory of his reign. However, in so doing, Belshazzar defiled sacred vessels by using them to serve wine to his Lords, his Wives, and his Concubines that they might "praise the gods of silver, and gold, of brass, iron, wood, and stone, which see not, nor hear, nor know." But then a mysterious Hand appears and writes on the wall: *Mene, Mene, Tekel, Upharsin.* The message is inscrutable to all present, so Belshazzar commands that Daniel be brought forth to decipher since Daniel is known to be skilled in such matters. Daniel deciphers the message to mean that Belshazzar's reign has come to an end, and that in the balance he has been found wanting, and that his kingdom will be divided between the Medes and the Persians. Being made aware of that presentiment effectively seals Belshazzar's doom. He dies that very night. And, figuratively, so it is also with any fanatic and his chimera when the latent meaning behind his obsessions becomes too evident though protectively ennobled they may be by claims of Ministry or Destiny. So too even with his followers when they come to see that the man behind the curtain is something less grand than their Hope demands, their loyalty thus cheapened. His more frenzied followers typically refute *that* kind of Change and usually become more dogged and desperate in their devotion, and too often bitterly so. It is sometimes a small step from folly to fanaticism, and a smaller one yet from fanaticism to depravity. A "Cult of Personality" almost never dies peacefully.

And perhaps that's exactly what we've seen happen to our government over the past few years in that yet another wretched symptom of Federal folly has cropped up, this one involving the Internal Revenue Service, already the average tax-paying citizen's most hated—and most feared—government agency. Previously, the citizen was likely to take some solace in his belief that basic rights ordained by our Constitution, plus reasonable application of the law, afforded some protection against that ravenous Federal Leviathan. But when it happens that the very Chief of that agency, at the direction of the Oval Office (read President Barack Obama) uses the power of that agency to target individual citizens and groups for partisan reasons alone then we cannot help but know that our nation, certainly the Federal sector of it, has sunk to the level of Third World tyranny. Such is another glaring indicator of the great leveling effect pursued by this Administration, though perhaps a level more coarse and gross than intended. But, then, voter base just about always has the last word on political as well as civic style. Indeed, the larger part of the work force of that indicted agency is drawn from the Administration's own voter base. Hence, ready compliance with such abuse of power is, with suitable supervisory direction, immediately at hand for partisan use and likely reflects the extent of corruption as may be brought to bear for implementing any renegade policy within the Capitol's precincts.

The upshot of the IRS scandal is that it has created a Constitution crisis. The very government mandated by the Constitution, defined by the Constitution, empowered by the Constitution is being suborned by partisan forces to deny citizens the very rights and protections ordained by the Constitution itself, and the citizenry is bound by Federal law to fund the very agency driving those encroachments. This is tyranny, and it is also bondage of the most execrable stripe, save slavery itself. And that may not be totally coincidental. We know that President Obama has no respect for the Constitution other than perhaps recognizing it as a finely articulated engine of government which requires skill, subtlety, and a large measure of nether power to subvert, and as such stands as a formidable obstacle to those who would recast our government in the shape of their own image and agenda. Such has been tried before, history will tell us if asked, and our Constitution bears the wear marks of previous such encounters though its essential structure remains intact. But the electorate, not so finely articulated, does indeed change, and not always in its own best interests, don't we know, and usually it quite unwittingly becomes a recruit in movements to re-fashion our government better to accommodate newly acquired and quite questionable pursuits such as importing "undocumented" Mexicans to trim our lawns, or programs distributing condoms to school children. Such emollients enlarge the voter rolls in a direction generative of not only enlarged government but also unbridled governmental participation in the lives of *all* citizens—President Obama's apparent modus operandi in its essential nature. Plus a majority of our Congressional caucus, for reasons partisan as well as personal, sustain the effort. To those congenial to Change at any cost, such colluding sentiments offer the opportunity and means of generating partisan momentum for the softening of firmly foundationed Imperatives, such as Amendments, into more malleable and negotiable accommodations, and all in the name of improving government efficiency and the focusing of its effectiveness—window dressing for power and control.

The upshot of dismantling our institutions in order to suit them to a different orientation and altered purpose while our general legal codes remain relatively unchanged and derivative of our traditional governmental design grants large sway to malfeasance, bumbling incompetence, and especially temporizing dissimulation. How so? Firstly, President Obama has surrounded himself with those who are ideologically kindred to himself, as Presidents do. Beyond the avowed anarchists, bomb-throwing activists, and the civil disobedients of his earlier years, President Obama has brought forth to high-level, even Cabinet position, people whose ideology and agendas have flourished in the shadows for many years, persons known to each other, but protected from public visibility by secrecy, stealth, and even in some cases, the sanction of college faculties. These people have in common a hatred of this nation, and they share the goal of overthrowing the government as founded, and instituting

215

some Socialist (read Communist) regime in its place. But enervating our government as founded and currently in place, especially its exceptionalism, becomes the crucial and unavoidable first step for doing so. In keeping with their sinister and alien aspect, these people earlier approached this task with open violence, such as blowing up buildings, robbing banks and other criminal behaviors appropriate to their status in the larger society, marking clearly the distinction between their ideology's self-accommodating morality and that of the civic-based general populace. Some of these activists later, from their college lecterns, lamented not destroying more, human life included if thought necessary. This barbarous assault upon the civil sector, directed and implemented from outside the established government, saw no repentance at any time, but merely went underground when pursued and remained there, nourished by covert sympathizers until a more propitious day arrived.

That day came when President Obama was elected. Those activists, along with their supporters, emerged into the open and were appointed to various government positions to form an operational cadre to serve as pivotal enablers in his Administration. The assault upon this nation had thus undergone a seminal change: now, the government as constituted was to be destroyed from *within*, aided by the ready assistance of electoral naiveté coupled with partisan abasement, and the whole of it perversely enabled by the very freedoms our Constitution guarantees to all. Moreover, the work of demolition is saluted as the means of sharing the wealth.

But not entirely. President Obama's election and re-election is unavoidably seen as at least this nation's good faith demonstration of man's equality under the law and the categorical rejection of the evils of Racism. Not only is he the first Black Chief Executive of a world power, but the freely elected leader of the world's greatest power, thanks to the fair-mindedness of the American people. A racist society would never have permitted that, no matter the extent of voter fraud assistance. As such, it is a global triumph of Democracy as practiced in this nation.

But it's not seen quite that way by President Obama and his followers, especially his most ardent voter base. It's not seen as exemplary of this nation's dedication to open government of, for, and by the people, but rather as defeat of an enemy using restrictive documents to oppress a long-suffering and disadvantaged minority. No, President Obama and his following do not see his victory as that of a duly appointed aspirant for elected office in a lawful and democratic referendum in which the free will of the people, by simple majority, chose its leader. No, that would be the mark of *National* thinking by which this republic provides the wherewithal for its citizens to choose as they wish. No, President Obama and his followers think not of a national process to be honored, but of *enemies* to be destroyed. Reverence for *National* identity does not figure largely in his camp. Nor does conjoint citizenship of the populace whose differences are to be sounded in open forum for possible consensus. Moreso, the political milieu is seen as a matter of friends or enemies, winner take all. One will seldom hear President Obama, in his rhetoric, speak of "us Americans," or "we citizens of this great nation," or "our revered founders," much less "our pride in being the inhabitants of so glorious a country as we Americans have." No, the nation is seen as a battle ground with political strife the order of the day. There may be mention of compromise now and again, but it is invariably tactical and disingenuous rather than consentient. No, the daily setting is of struggle between race and/or class, openly or covertly joined; to the victor goes the spoils, and losers are to be eliminated. Quite Marxian, and quite dependent on perduring conflict necessary to the nature of the system whose dialectic depends on there being an enemy at hand always; specifically, any thesis (government, process, social structure, etc.) has to have an antithesis (reformer, activism, revolution, etc.) in order for there to be a synthesis for the establishment of a new thesis (equality of need and use of resources in production, etc.). Take Soviet Russia. In its seventy-five years of existence it was never without an explicating enemy, either within or without, often both, and it never ceased courting additional ones, as its dialectic demanded, for perpetuation of its political existence. The thinking is innately *Tribal*, not national; the method is *Conquest*, not collaboration; and the goal is *Loot,* not enterprise—all in the name of Peace come of "spreading the wealth." Also, we are witnessing the rank and file of the government plundering the national treasury while President Obama himself sets that very tone by his total disregard for any pretense to a continent or decorous Presidential lifestyle. He now lives a life of imperial splendor, exceeding by far that of the emperors of old, even that of Belshazzar himself, one supposes. Friends and followers are richly favored in all dealings while other citizens' efforts to call attention to such abominations are suppressed by the very governmental agencies sharing in the imperial largess. The country's landscape has become one in which national wealth, created by the people throughout the land, has been concentrated in Washington with the White House and its inhabitants as its epicenter, the national wealth to be skimmed as needed at the pleasure of the government and its personnel, leaving the nation's housekeeping bills to the energies and productivity of the more enterprising and functional everyday citizens. Very tribal.

However, the pool of enterprising and functional citizens is not keeping pace with the growth of the national debt. Indeed, the ratio of productive to custodial populace is, apparently by design, decreasing in keeping with President Obama's management of our Mexican Border and our proven but now politically inconvenient immigration policy. The trickledown effect of such, coupled with President Obama's economic policy, has resulted in sustained high unemployment rates, correspondingly record numbers of people on unemployment compensation, soaring numbers of disability claimants, endless lines at the Welfare office, and minuscule growth in the Gross National Product. Yet, oddly and contrary to what the simple citizen would expect, these shortfalls are not out of keeping with the larger design of President Obama's grand agenda. By and large the people endemic to such civics belong to his standard voter base, and those who are new entries to the work force in the face of our blunted economy will likely find themselves also obliged to seek some measure of government assistance, such as food stamps, for mere subsistence. Hence, President Obama's call to "spread the wealth"—beginning at the top as promised—likely would offer some measure of "Hope" to such economically benighted. After all, he seems to hold that everything – truly everything – ultimately belongs to the government, and that the purpose of rule is to determine who gets what and how much. The individual worker continues to be the producer but is to have little say so beyond that. And certainly this appeals to a very large sector of his voter base, and, perhaps, even beyond as long as it is not seen by too many people as our having to take a large step backward to a lesser life style, likely Second or even Third World life style (read Detroit). But the standard media will stand available to smooth the rough edges of reality and help with recruitment.

It would seem then, that despite pro forma protestations to the contrary, an anemic economy is essential to the nourishment of President Obama's voter base and, consequently, the effectiveness and success of his grand agenda. Thus, the oil boom come of the engineering miracle of fracking is seen by him and his following as a malady to be contained by whatever means possible. The threat it poses is not to the environment, but to him and his design for changing our government. True, the conventional wisdom, recited most by the standard media, is the canard that the Environmentalist movement is so very strong and that the President works so very hard at achieving a compromise with its following in hope of salvaging the benefits of such drilling success when, in truth, the Environmentalists are his canny political ally in preventing private enterprise from restoring a vibrant, free, and *open* economy. It is in his agenda's best interest, as has been said, to keep the economy in a state of crisis. It's also an easy prediction that he will never sign approval of the Canadian Keystone pipeline, and his explanation will include an accounting of the Environmentalist lobby as a most formidable advocate in protecting the natural beauty of the land along with its endangered fauna and flora, and that his best efforts certainly have to take those commendable sentiments into account. Cynicism and dissimulation at their obfuscating best. The resulting and very prohibitive regulations, in their vast plentitude, exert a paralyzing effect on vitalizing enterprises, such as that pipeline, and are the intended progeny of his administration, and, specifically the issue of his own thinking. The Environmentalists likely are willing to play the rôle of Horatius at the Bridge in this tryst—the more to their credit, they must feel—but, again, the man behind the teleprompter behind the curtain is the President himself.

Also, President Obama is dedicated to keeping America dependent on the Middle East for oil. He is likely Muslin in the deeper springs of his soul—his wife has suggested as much in an unguarded comment—and he would have no problem with American money being used to fund the growth and spread of Islamic society. After all, he does bow to its kings. Humbling America in kind would likely add an especially gratifying wrinkle in doling out condign punishment, as he sees it, to an arrogant America which took war to a Muslim country. Middle East Oil, we suspect he believes, should continue as a prominent means by which America remains dependently respondent to the wishes of certain other favored nations. And Israel would best beware.

The evolving scandals cited above "will not remove nor choke the strong conception" be clearly seems to groan withal: he is determined to punish this nation for its sins (read Slavery), and its hubris (read Power and Exceptionalism), and he is fortifying his cabinet and fellow travelers with vast increases in authority to accomplish just that. These measures are generally at the expense of, plus are designed to restrict, personal rights and liberties guaranteed under our Constitution. His use of Executive Privilege as a device for circumventing Congress, and hence the will of the American people, is signal in his style of office, and thus a steady erosion of personal freedom in favor of centralized control and regulation in all aspects of the citizen's life is daily at hand. To some, if not most of his electorate, such a change in civic status is not unacceptable if balanced by a promised, off-setting increase in protection from the vagaries of ordinary living since such persons generally do not make much use of opportunity or their liberty other than to petition government for more benefits which they feel are to be given, not earned. However, most Americans still prefer to have the opportunity and liberty to pursue their own fortunes and not settle for what a government bureaucracy decides a citizen is allowed to have. But this preference is contingent expressly upon having the opportunity to pursue such fortunes free of government infringement. The mounting fear of government currently conveyed by the people is that the rapid expansion of government and its insinuation into the personal lives of all will, *pari passu*, indent specifically the individual's freedom to seek his own fortunes come of applying his own energies and talents to the betterment of his own life and that of his family.

But if the path of government has indeed diverged from the wishes of, for, and by the people, why can't it be returned to its constituted purpose? Because President Obama is simply not amenable to such, and a predominantly self-serving Congress has no stomach for the task of restoring it so. Then why can't the people demand impeachment, gross malfeasance being demonstrably at hand? Simply stated, because he's Black. Assuredly, any White President guilty of the same dissemblance, out-and-out lying, and abuse of executive power would readily be impeached. But not President Obama, and he knows it. Being Black makes him untouchable. His lieutenants may be fired, sanctioned, cited, and so forth, but they accept such risks knowing that their leader is functionally sovereign and will protect them. And he does, though an occasional sacrificial firing may become at times politically necessary. But why does his being Black make him invulnerable? Several reasons, probably the simplest of which is that many Americans just don't want to face the harsh fact that they, in good faith, made a grievous mistake in electing to the highest office in the land someone who had the covert agenda of changing this county into something the large majority of its citizens do not want and never would have voted to have, had they known his true agenda. And no one likes to be recognized as having been made a fool of, or of having placed our proud and wondrous nation in such jeopardy, as spoiled and irresponsible children might. The "good faith" aspect of their deed was that they trusted President Obama to be color blind in the performance of his duties, and such has not proven to be the case at all. Black, threatening, election-eering thugs, for example, go unprosecuted. Had they been White they likely would still be in jail.

But more than even that misbegotten hope, White America does indeed have a collective sense of guilt over its fellow Black citizens. No living White American is guilty of Slavery, for sure, but the engram is there for Whites to register *any* unfavorable thoughts or feelings they may have about Blacks as kindred to the Racism generative of Antebellum Slavery and the subsequent Jim Crow period. Monumental remedial effort has been made by White America over the past half century to undo the injustices of those earlier times and elevate thereby the Black man to social and industrial parity with the White man. Today Black America, the world's largest Black enfranchised population living in a pre-dominantly non-Black industrialized and technologically advanced nation, enjoys the highest standard of living among Blacks anywhere else. Still and all, this counts for little in Black American political rhetoric, even though stark Black preference is widely and dutifully practiced in academia, the work place, and especially in govern-mental funding allocation. Still, the "race card" is never out of play; in no small way it is a useful device for refreshing the White sense of guilt should any unrest arise because of grossly unfair practices— such as *reverse* Racism—come of Affirmative Action zeal. White America seems to have no defense whatever against the charge of Racism even when there is a patently just case against current Black transgressions. And thus it is likewise with President Obama himself and his frank malfeasances and dissimulations. Plus, the standard media remains available to fill the air with the melodies of Stephen Foster as suitable accompaniment.

Why no defense? Because, regrettably there is a basic misconception busily at play at all times in the American populace—maybe especially in White America—and this regrettable misconception is a flawed understanding of the difference between the terms *Racist* and *Racial*, which takes us back to the very first entry of this collection to which the reader is referred for a more specific discussion. But for the nonce, *Racist*, or *Racism*, involves *unfairness* while *Racial* is merely descriptive of an objective observation noting distinguishing features. "He is a stupid Black" is certainly a towering and inflammatory *racist* remark. In contrast, "He is a Black Man who often does less well in the standard educational setting than do Whites and Orientals" is a *racial* comment. The latter is an objective, essentially neutral statement of observed fact, as regrettable as it is, while the former is a maliciously intended denigration precasting judgment. Not only is it hateful, but, worse, it is also unwarranted, unfair, and thus *racist*. But what about "The Black race, of its own and aside from assimilation, has shown over the thousands of years of human history the least cultural development of all races, and thus suffers inordinately in the modern mix of Man because of this deficiency, and hence finds itself regrettably dependent on the more culturally, industrially, and technologically advanced races for sustaining its membership in modern world society." Just about everybody would feel uncomfortable with so bold a statement and, if forced to call it, would likely label it as *racist*. But why *racist* when it is merely an observation which squares fairly well with observable fact? Because we Americans, especially we non-Black Americans, have been rigorously trained to think so out of deference to Black sensitivity on the matter. Branded as *racist*, the observation is banned. Yet, it is a common sense fact observable to all, and though it is before us at all times we are forbidden to admit its existence. In effect, we have to deny what our

223

own common sense tells us. If we covertly persist in knowing the truth of the matter we are covertly nourishing a secret *racism*, as current American social and political policy demands we "correctly" see it, one might say. It is this *alleged* racism, fraudulent though the charge may be, which stokes White guilt; and the White man, blessed as everyone else with God-given common sense, is required to forsake that vital faculty to escape the charge of *racism*. And he can't, and remain functionally sane. So, in our current lexicon of Political Correctness, sanity, common sense, and the *courage* to account them their due, is coupled with *Racism*. To avoid being charged so, we have no choice but to endorse the tender, poignant, but patent adolescent nonsense that we are all essentially equal and that any consequential differences between us are man-made and therefore evil and curable by legislation. Just like global warming. Our Founding Fathers knew where to draw the line on this matter of equality: *equal under the law* and nowhere else since no two people are exactly alike, as even identical twins know. In our all too human way of reckoning, maybe a non-partisan Evolution hasn't been quite "fair" to the Black race, but such a notion would not make much hay if worked into our political rhetoric, since most of our politicians are regrettably more all too human than even their constituents, but it just might free up energy from the internecine sideshow we call the American political scene to allow for framing the problem more clearly and perhaps favoring a less symptomatic and more opera- tionally-defined approach for addressing the problem in its genuine reality. But taboo has such deep roots. Tribalism, too. Perhaps political depravity deepest of all. And we need not be reminded that nobody ever became depraved suddenly.

So what of the future?

We are fully aware that detailing the national political scene as we see it, applying our speculations as to the intent and purpose of President Obama's enactments, yields the impression that we believe he is attempting a massive and, thus far, relatively bloodless coup. Such a notion may seem excessive, but to us the indicators do not appear to stack up any other way. A bit of transparency would help just now. There is a widespread, poorly articulated sense that this nation is losing something vital to its existence as the world's beacon of liberty; our proud statue on Bedloe's Island is at very great risk of becoming nothing more in its meaning than a quaint tourist attraction. Indeed, it seems that the most progressive element, one might say, of our current political scene is a widespread popular disenchantment: one political faction is grating in its Deliverance Apologetics (read Democrat), while the other faction is resolutely paretic in its Establishment Propriety (read Republican). And the people, in their daily duty and toils, sustain the essence of Nation while Washington spins tangent to the meaning of America. Where is *our* Daniel— White, Black, Yellow, or Red—to decipher the moment and discern *our* way? What is the antidote to our present national distemper? President Obama has been found wanting, but he can only be what he is. Yet, in the theme of Blackness, Providence has quite possibly delivered Hope in the form of several other Black men who could, we think, stand good the better reach of not only our Black citizens, but of *all* Americans, and that these men could, we suspect, join with our rising White statesmen new to the national horizon, and together, with a better informed electorate, one not quite so heavy with those who see not, nor hear, nor know, restore this nation to its glory as the land of the exceptionally free.

15 June 2013

XXIX

Bread and Circuses

In November, 2012, despite our economy being in stagnation, unemployment soaring, and the national debt climbing to unbelievable heights, the American people, acting affirmatively and thus divorcing honest assessment of performance from its grim reality, elected President Barack Obama to a second term. President Obama chose to conduct his re-election campaign via late night and morning TV talk show performances, knowing full well that his voter base much preferred to be entertained rather than be informed or educated. Eschewing the usual venues past presidents have used to convey their positions and policies to the public, he instead chatted amiably with fawning talk show hosts, who either did not have the capacity to ask relevant questions or the courage to challenge his obvious distortions of the truth, or both.

The lap-dog mainstream media, print and electronic, no longer make any pretense of disguising their drooling devotion to President Obama. The motto of one notable newspaper used to be "All the news that's fit to print." Now, a more apt motto would be, "All the news that fits." Our Founding Fathers saw a free press as vital to maintaining our hard-won liberty by keeping a vigilant and watchful eye on elected officials who might abuse their power. The modern, mainstream media no longer see it as their bounden duty to seek and report the truth—regardless of where it leads—so that the electorate can make informed and sound decisions in choosing leaders.

Clearly, most of the media today share President Obama's agenda of Social Engineering, and thus they slant their reports to portray him in the most favorable light and readily depict critics who oppose his ruinous policies as racists and bigots. In order to keep a

227

lid on the escalating scandals of his administration, the mainstream media tries to bury the unacceptable news of the day under a mountain of trivia about the First Lady's new hairdo, celebrity gossip, fashion faux pas of the rich and famous, use of performance enhancing drugs by sports figures, or just plain old freak show oddities. Stories of this stripe were the mainstay of what used to be known as Yellow Journalism.

Another tactic such media uses to take the public attention off banned news of national importance is to latch on to a local tragic event and turn it into a nonstop media Circus. The media vultures seem to relish picking at the remains of the victims of the tragedy and the fresh wounds of their survivors. This 24/7 news feeding-frenzy on local tragic events seems to have a not so coincidental tendency to surface when the Obama Administration is trying to downplay its latest scandal. Quite Yellow.

The more telling evidence of the mainstream media's liberal bias lies in the news they choose not to report; i.e., the attack on the Benghazi Consulate, the targeting of Tea Party members by the IRS, the NSA secret data-gathering on average American citizens, the "Fast and Furious" gun-running fiasco on our southern border, and the grisly Gosnell abortion clinic murders of live-born babies.

Hence, stories with a racial component are suppressed only if they involve Black on White crime. If the alleged perpetrator is White and the victim is Black the rush to judgment is lightning-fast, and the verdict is always "guilty" before the trial has even begun. In keeping with the agenda of President Obama, his Attorney General, and certain notorious race-baiters, the mainstream press continues to promote the idea that America is a nation of White racists. It seems to have escaped their notice that President Obama could not have been elected President if that were true. They continue to advance this false premise even to the point of ruthlessly hounding a man who was found not guilty of murder in the killing of a young Black man, but acting only in self-defense. The man was found not guilty despite the U.S. Attorney General's meddling in this local matter by having a group of protestors convoyed to the site of the trial in order to sway the jurors against the defendant. This abuse of power by the Attorney General certainly did not receive wide coverage by the media.

One racial story which is never covered by the mainstream media is Black on Black crime. The carnage in the streets of Chicago, Barack Obama's hometown, rarely commands their attention other than to make brief mention of the weekly body count. Why is it that such an important story is neglected by the very media who purportedly has such great concern for our Black citizens? It would seem that if the blame for such savage behavior can't be shifted to elsewhere, it must be ignored or covered up since it just doesn't fit. Why isn't the President promoting real remedies for these problems, telling the Black youth that he himself is living proof that one can be anything one wants to be in America—if one works hard, gets an education, and takes responsibility for the children one brings into this world so that they, too, can have a better chance in life. This is a message that is never delivered by President Obama or the other race baiters; it's just not in their personal interest to do so. Instead of Hope, President Obama offers a message of Despair, telling Blacks that the cards are stacked against them and that they'll never get ahead without help from the government. The sad truth is that his policies are actually driving more and more people to a malignant dependency on government—a sure way to shackle the citizenry to his oppressive regime. Such bread!

Meanwhile the average American citizen seems to be resolutely ignorant of the cause of his daily discontent. It would be easy to blame the mainstream media because of its misfeasance in keeping the populace properly informed, but each and every one of us is personally responsible for keeping himself so informed. And it has never been easier to do so. Thanks to American ingenuity we have a wealth of information at our finger tips via computers and the internet. Unfortunately, these sources can't give us the will to inform and educate ourselves; they can only give us the means. Too many of us are content to fill our minds with trash, gorge ourselves on junk food, and cover our bodies with graffiti. To quote Juvenal, a Roman satirist who wrote before the collapse of the Roman Empire: "Only two things does he [the Roman citizen] anxiously wish for—bread and circuses." Will the people of this nation awaken to the perilous course this President has taken us on? If not, for us the writing will indeed be on the wall: America—Land of the Formerly Free.

02 September 2013

Envoi

With this collection of brief narratives we have attempted to present a sketch of the current American socio-political scene as we see it. In doing so we feel we have tapped into resources available to all citizens who might make a point of noting our nation's current socio-political predicament, its origins, its dialectic, and its apparent trajectory. We have tried to specify seminal points generative of the national milieu in which we now find ourselves, mindful that we all, as busy citizens, generally are no more inclined to be aware of the subtler, determinative forces which shape that milieu than is the fish aware of the water in which it swims, at least not until the water becomes significantly less habitable, as we fear is regrettably the case with our nation's current socio-political ambience. We have offered these pieces with differing degrees of elaboration and discussion in accordance with what we feel is the essential noteworthiness of their themes.

In that regard we have posited Race as a major element in our discussion in view of the profound influence we feel its political, social, and economic determinants have had, and, quite pointedly, continue to have on the forces shaping our American way of life. To wit, we now have our first Black President, but in that unique particular we have also the greatest degree of political and popular polarization since the Civil War. We have attempted to trace elements of our current national malaise to the festering residuals of that calamitous conflict, residuals rooted in and aggravated by the comparative and enduring culturally-challenged status of the Black race newly incarnated in the persona of President Obama himself and his private agenda which, in his pursuit of such, appears to transcend our founding documents in the scope of his sense of mission which we suggest is held by him to be messianic and ordained with its goal of lifting American Black society to a position of parity with the other racial groups of this nation whose acquired wealth would be more equably distributed to achieve such parity in satisfaction of a political ideology demonstrably inimitable with the political ideals for which this country is known and which have been generative of that very wealth.

We have also attempted to convey our belief that President Obama's geopolitical strategy, paralleling his domestic goals, bespeaks an effort to advance Islamic society to industrial-technologic parity with the prevalent Western world by dissolving political, military, and economic ties which are seen as traditionally having favored the latter. The incident at Benghazi qualifies as a tragic misstep in that pursuit. But here again the mission of "spreading the wealth" is evident with America scheduled to abandon its exceptionalism—and economic success—in favor of a more modest, consensually-based rôle on the world stage. We suspect these causes have their origins in crucial issues of his personal past which, by his own account, have imparted to him his sense of mission. Such may, in part, account for his having down-graded our military purpose in Afghanistan, a 99% Islamic country, to the status of a non-event.

We have also attempted to identify certain societal attitude changes which bear on national identity as well as individual responsibility as they relate to the rise of a pervasive cynicism regarding the meaning and message of our country. We see this cynicism as inviting a national decline readily accommodated by some of our political figures while vigorously opposed by others all the while too many of our general populace complacently abide, we feel, the prevailing partisan and too often self-serving themes issuing forth from our Capitol, the citizenry lately in lock step with our legislators' typically reckless and openly frivolous abuse of the national treasury.

As for the separate entries of this volume carrying dates, the purpose of such notation is to provide us with a record of the chronology of our thinking as we, individual citizens, experienced the remarkable and astonishing peculiarities of President Obama and his

Administration as they became more manifest along with the adumbration they carried. We see the dates as signifying our step-wise realization of what was nationally before us. We suspected that we were not alone in this experience but were, indeed, perhaps less encumbered in the frankness of these entries than some of our outspoken commentators using a medium which necessarily had to honor sponsor sensitivity as well as fiscal vulnerability. Never-theless, those commentators helped immeasurably in sustaining a tone of honest and objective inquiry, sort of like the water in which our thinking swam, and the currents they engendered pressed us onto the voyage this volume details. Our gratitude to those good captains of the airwaves is exceeded only by our esteem of their message, their dedication, and their courage. We hope that the reader of this volume can add his endorsement to that sentiment.

                            RMC
                            SWC

www.ingramcontent.com/pod-product-compliance
Lightning Source LLC
Chambersburg PA
CBHW030427290526
45786CB00001B/175